This book is mine

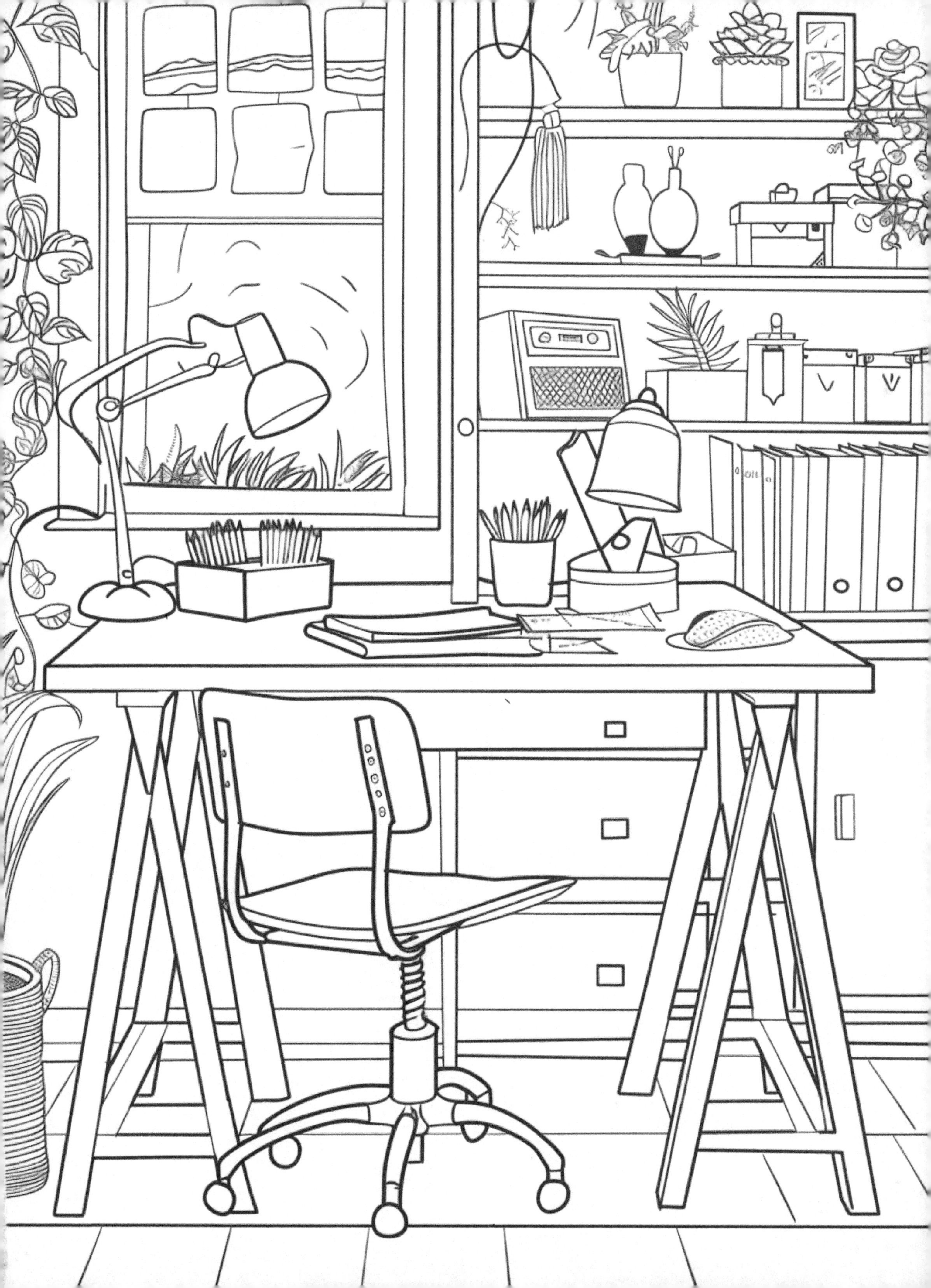

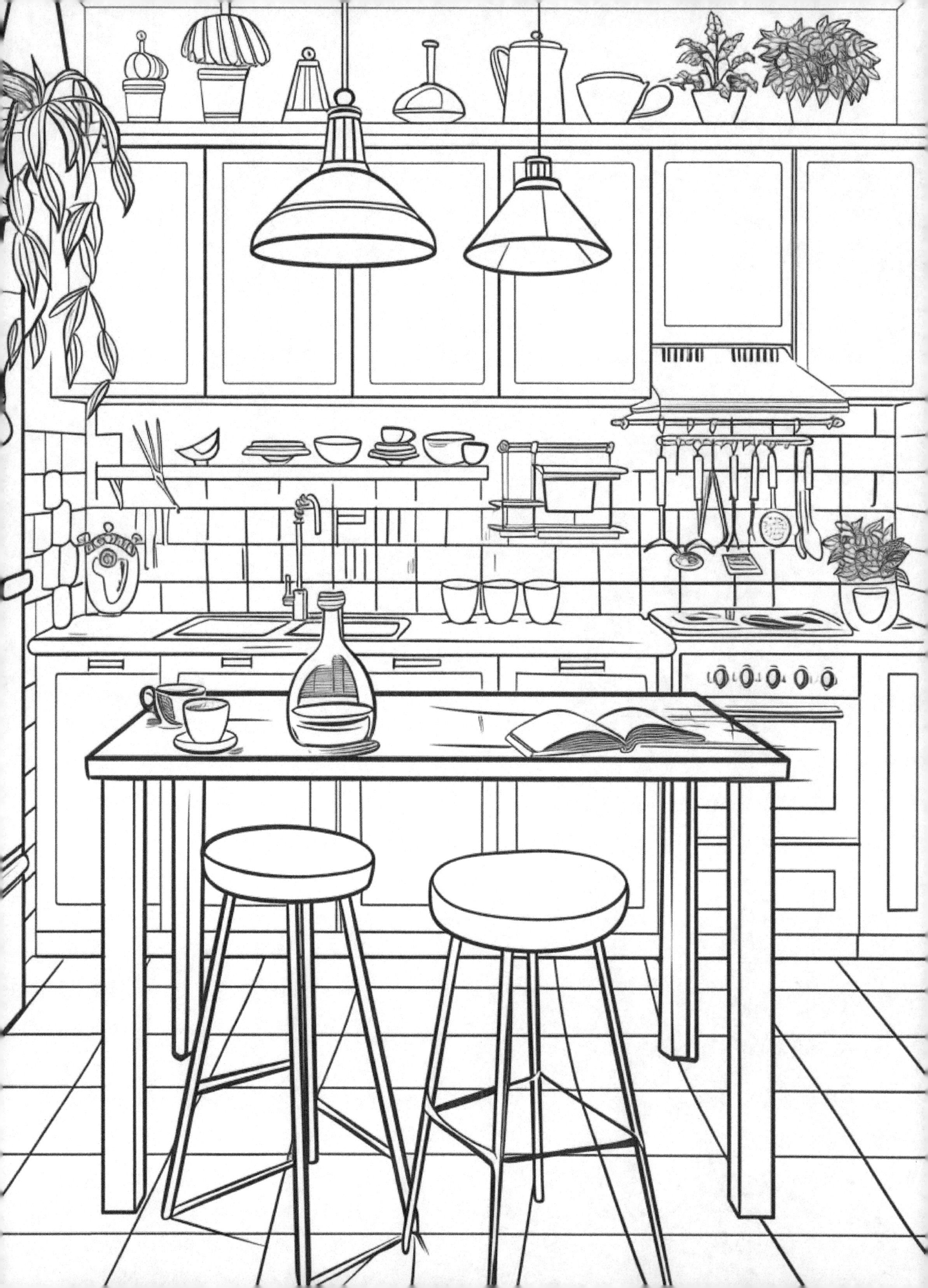

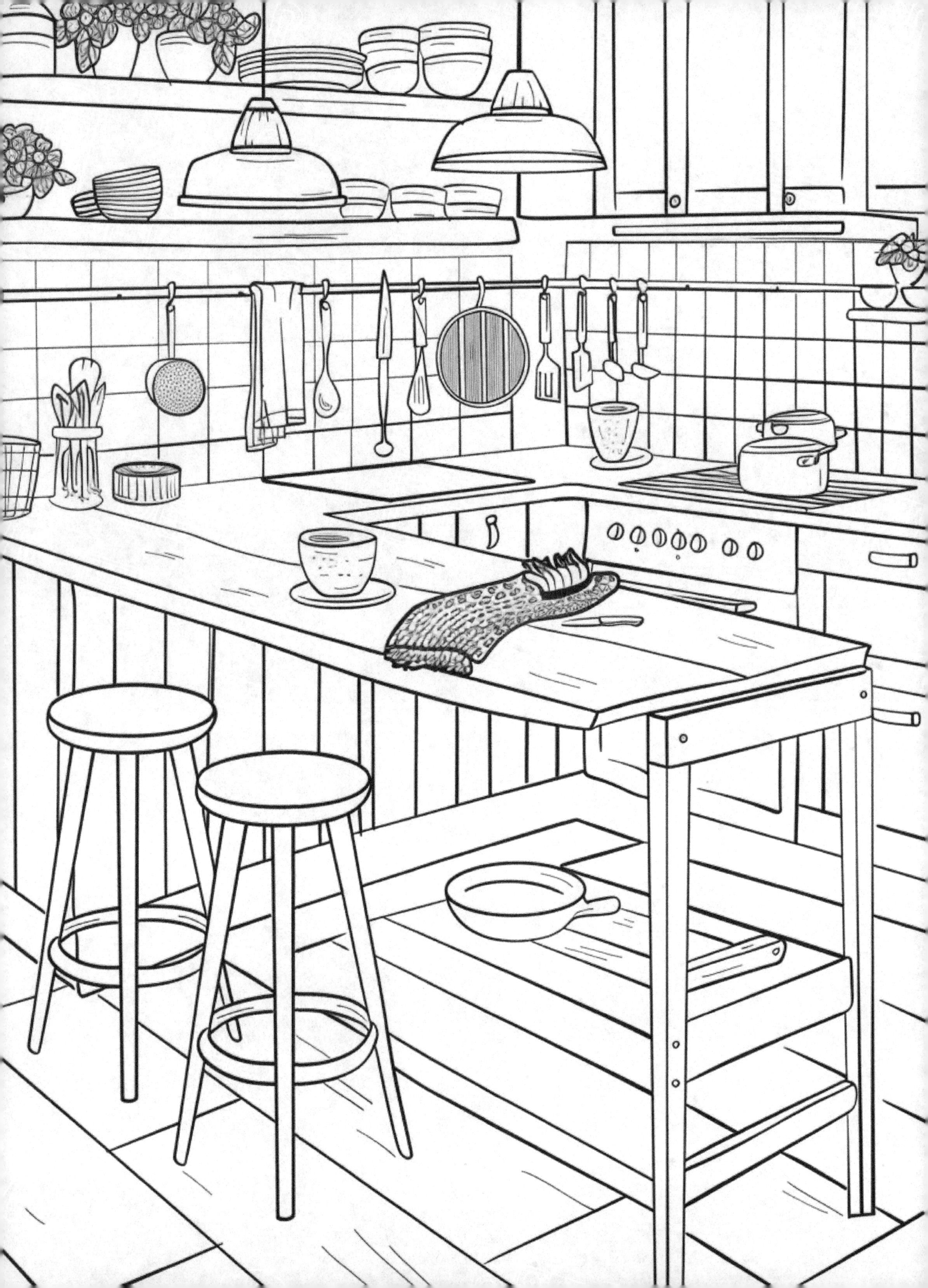

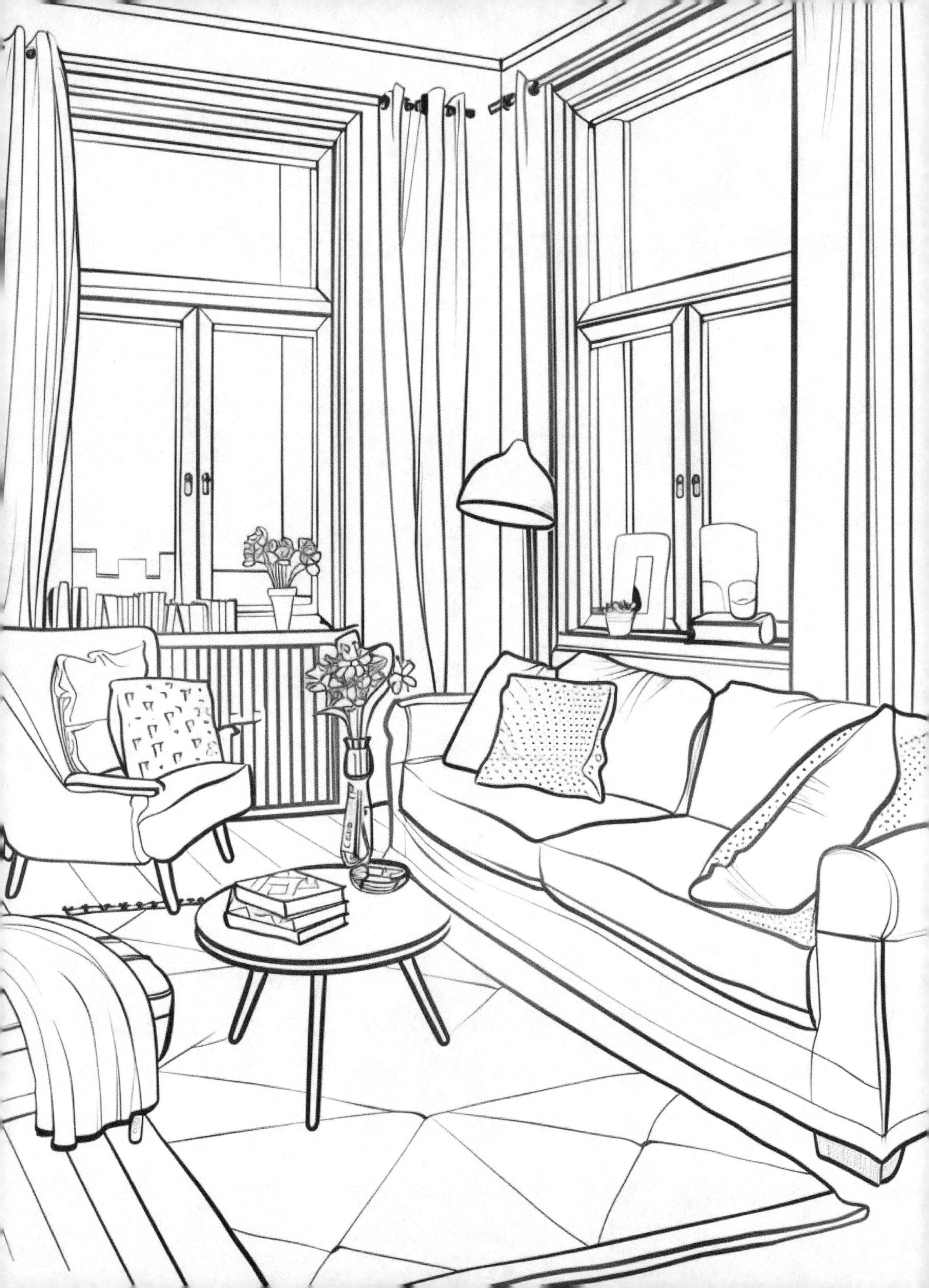

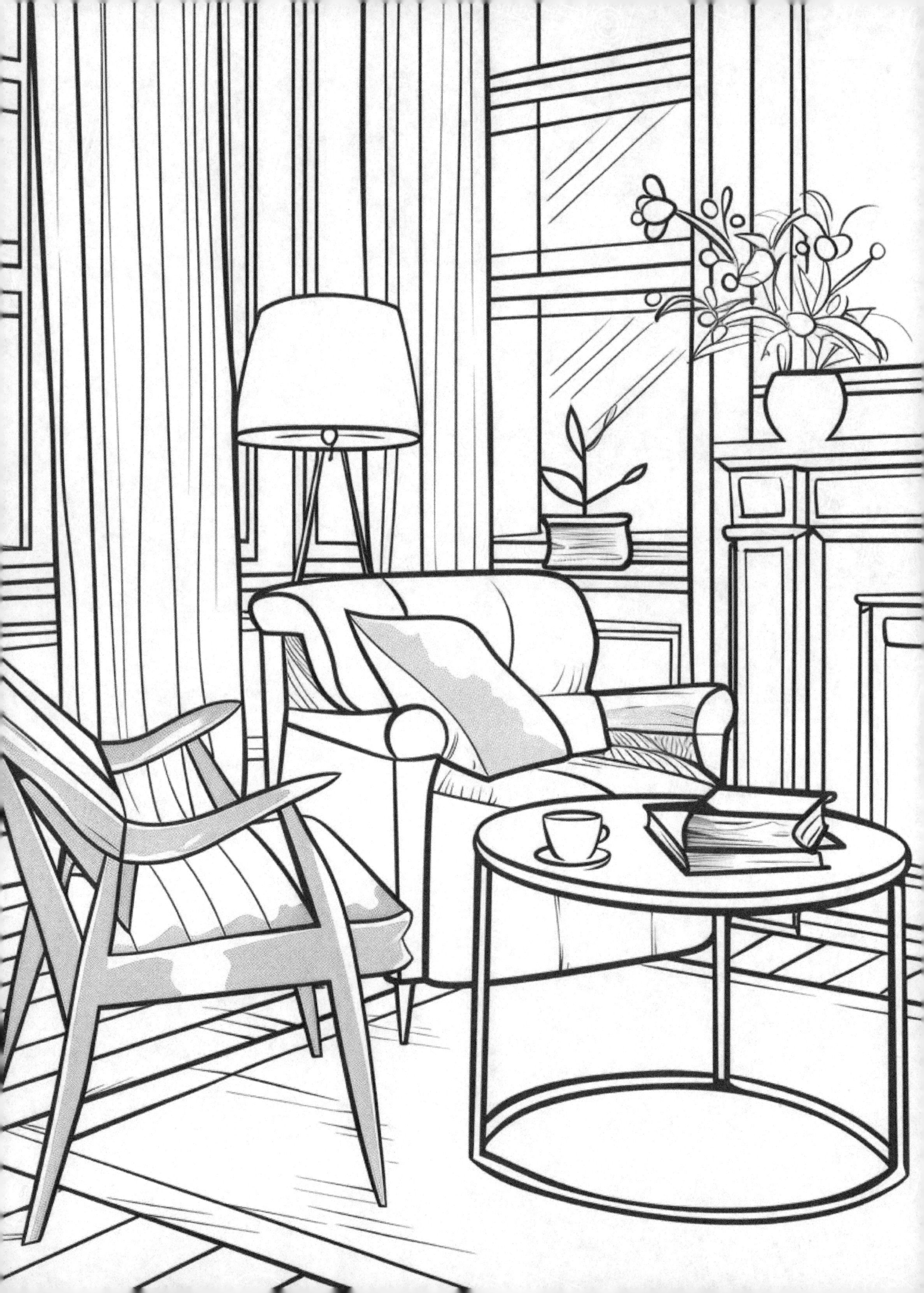

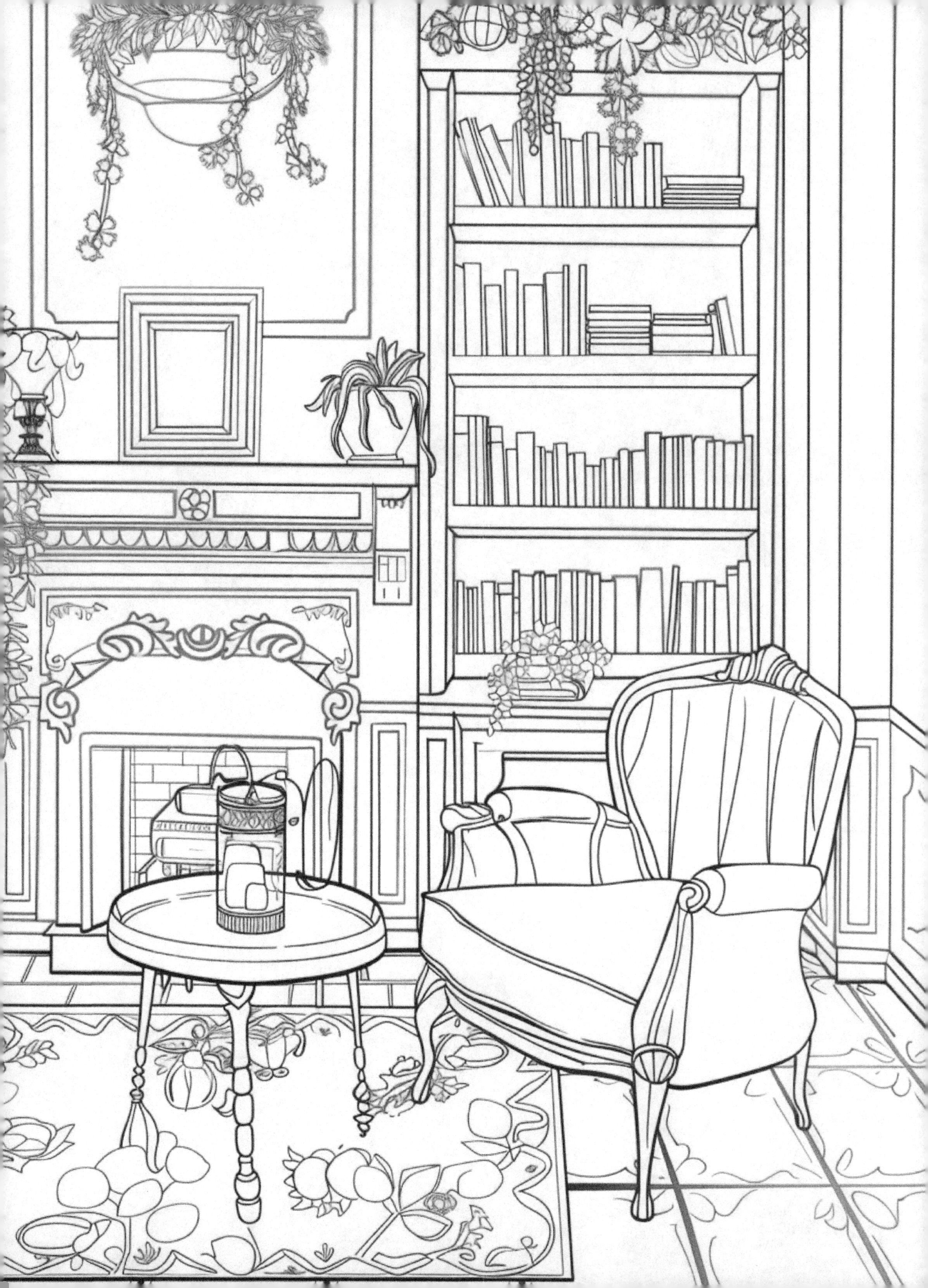

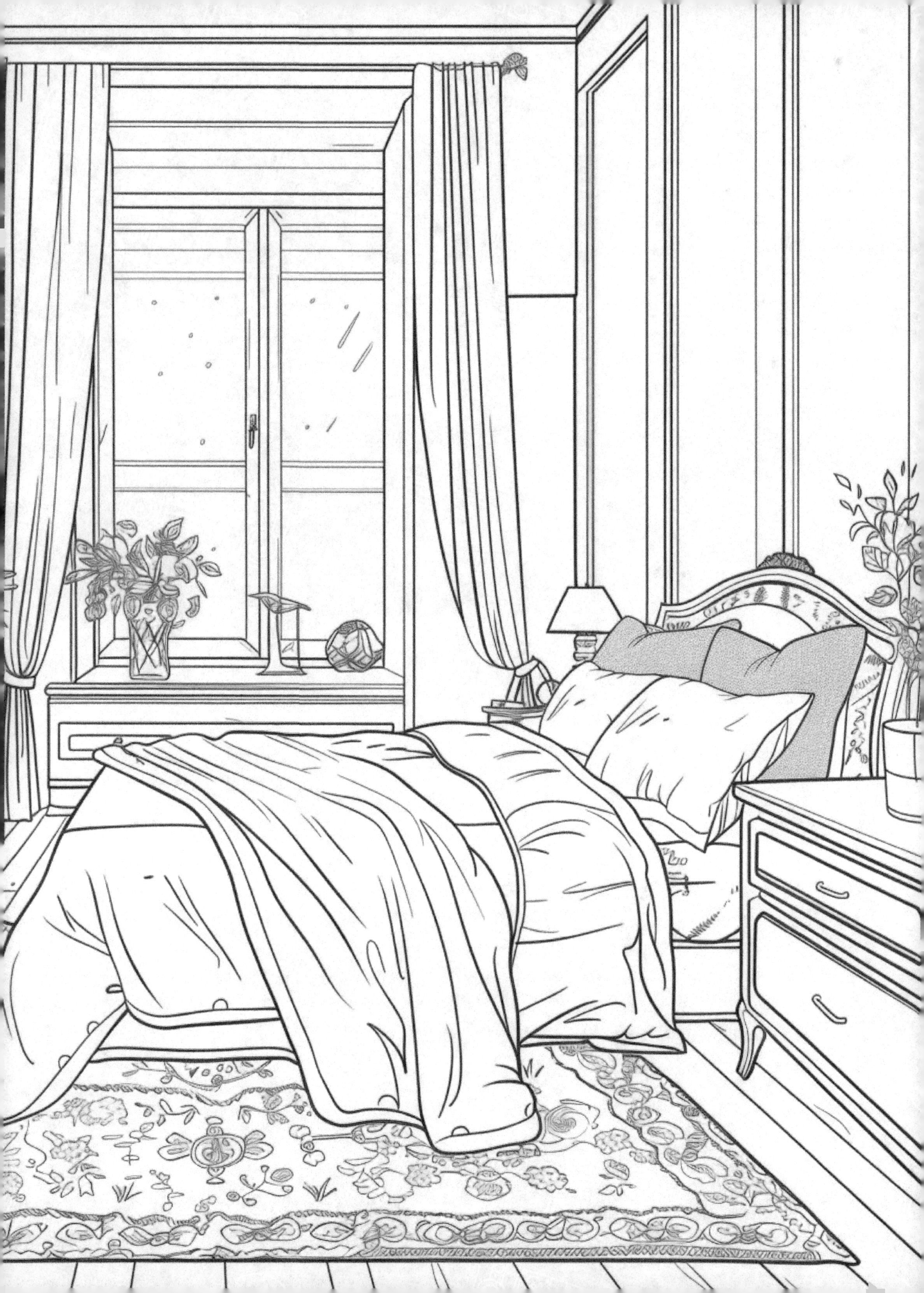

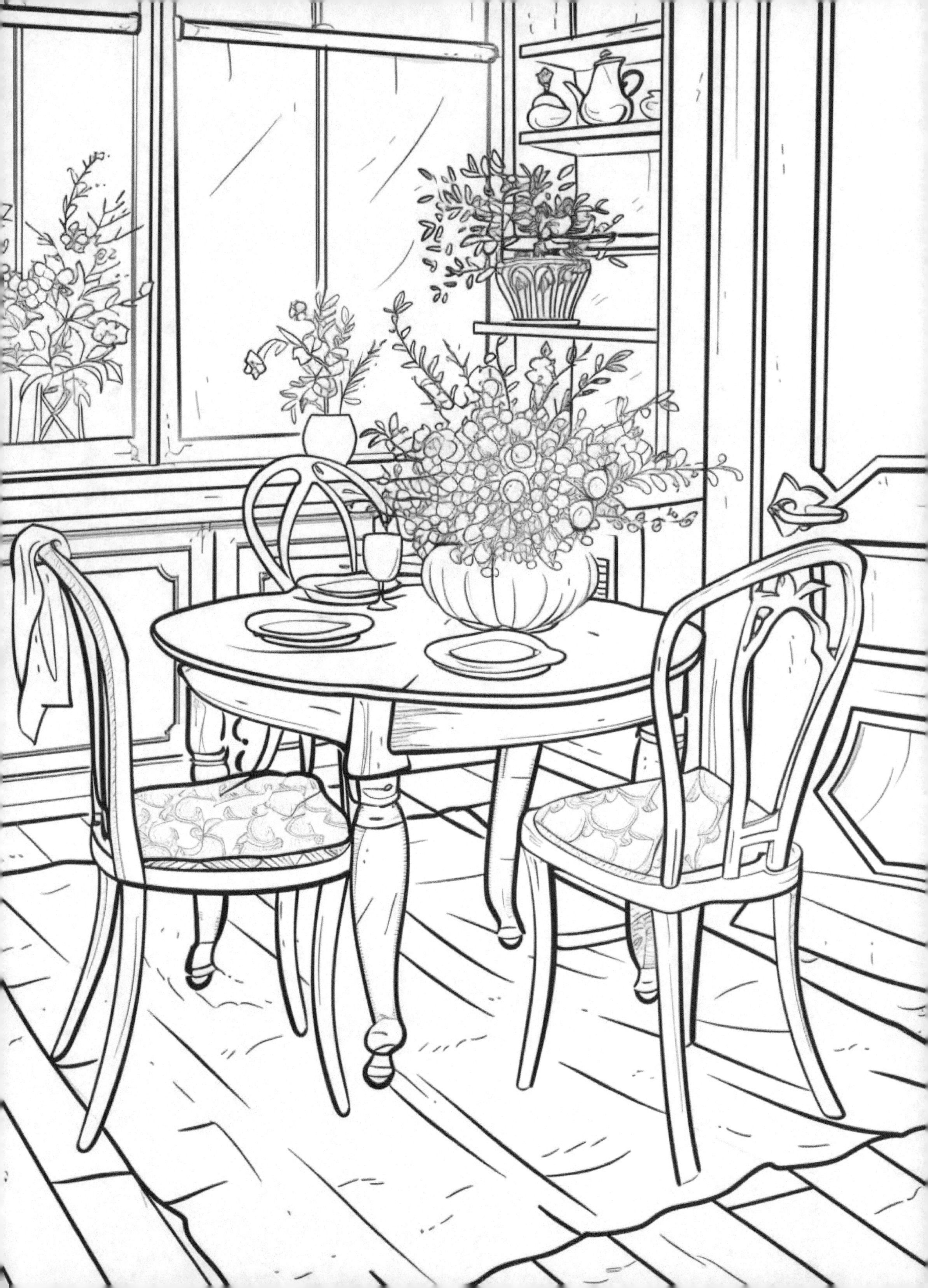

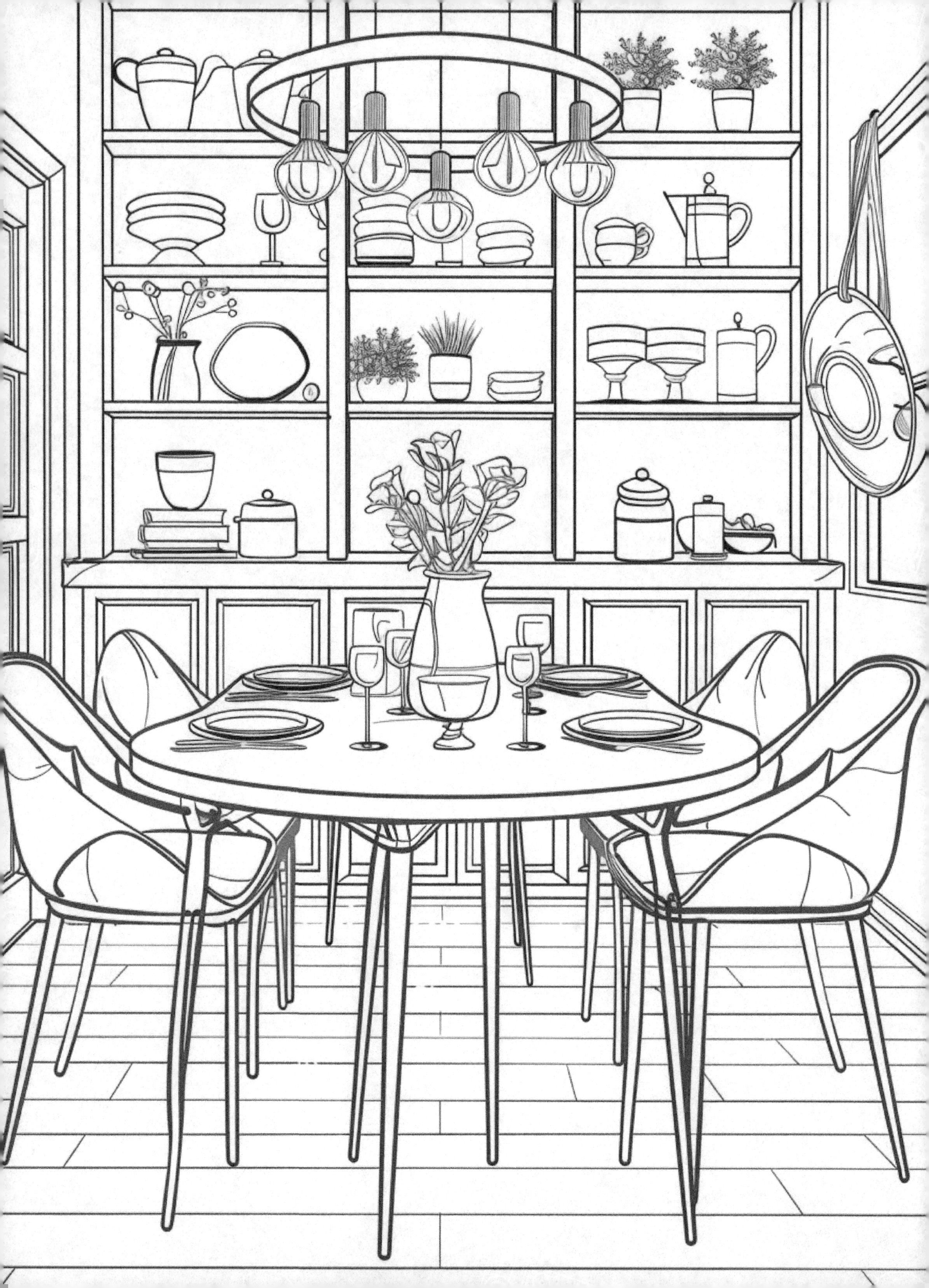

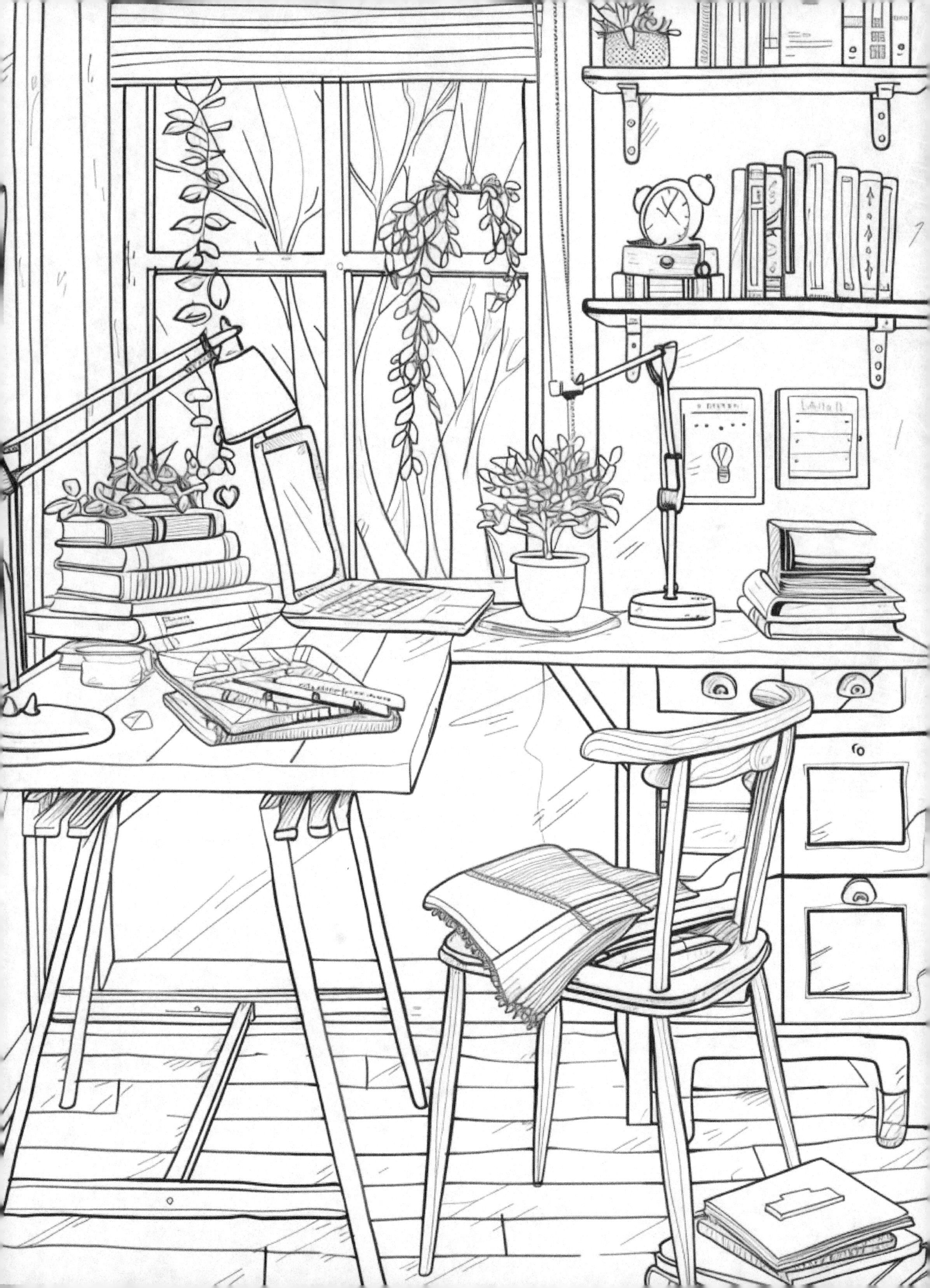

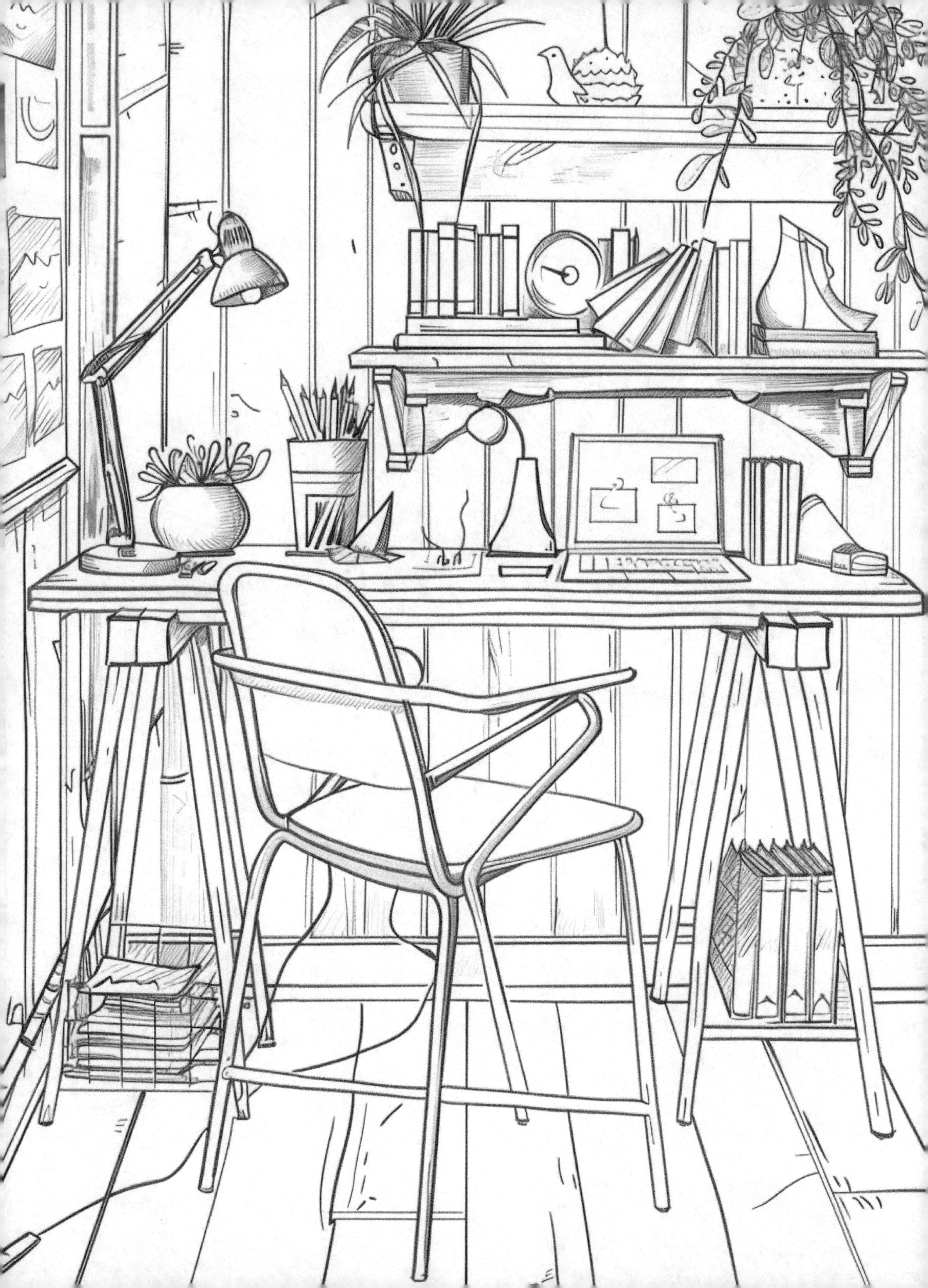

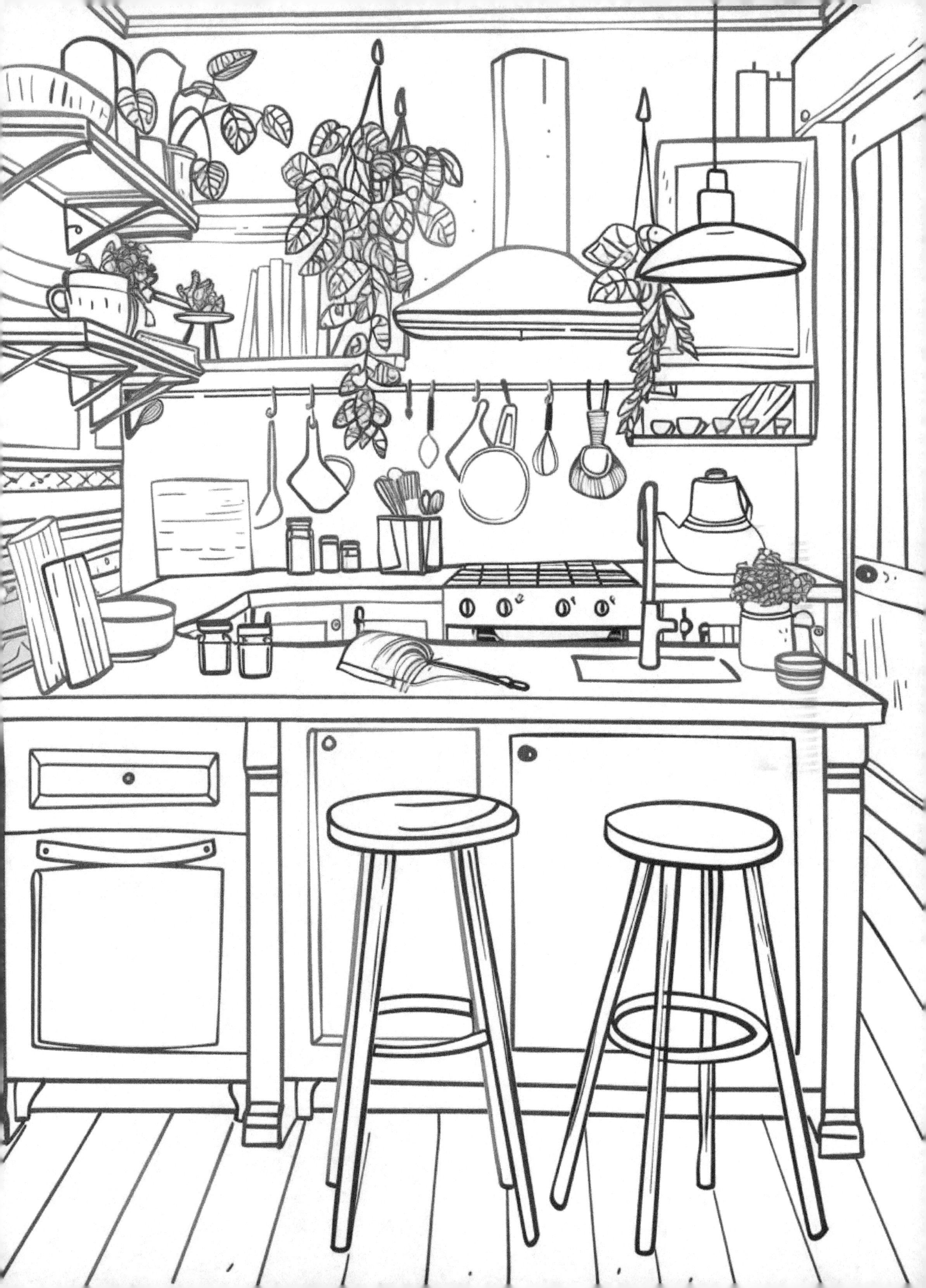

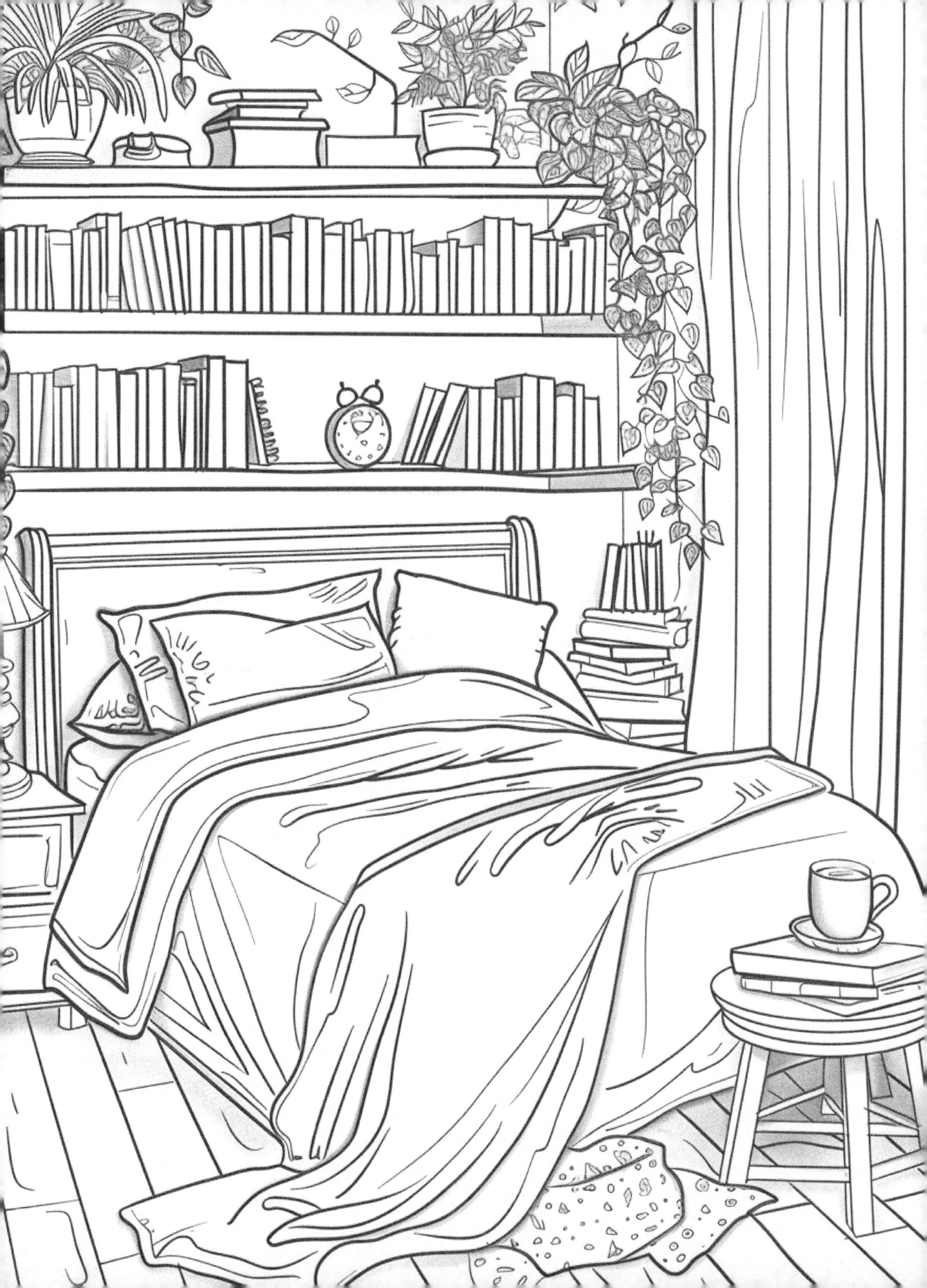

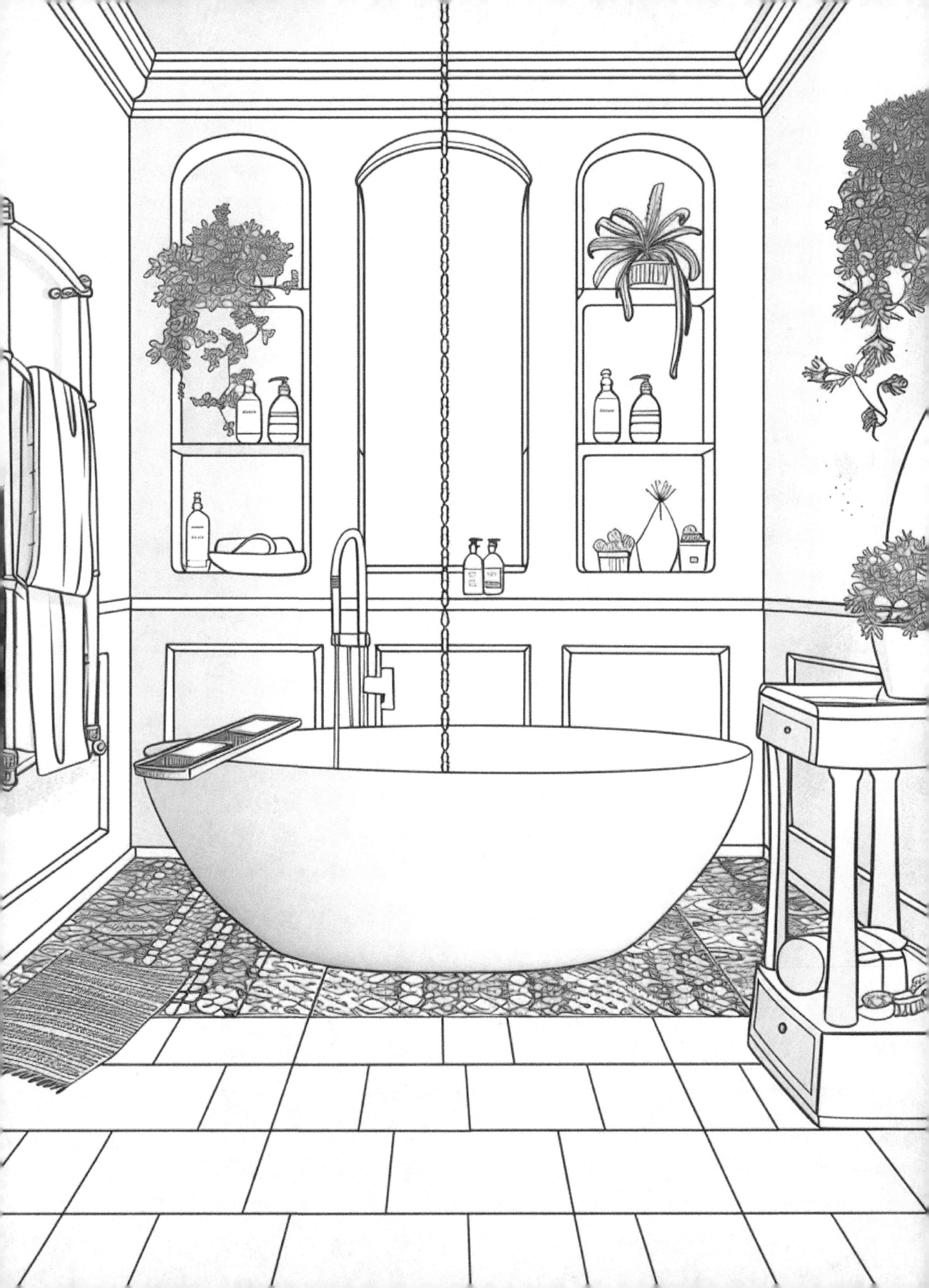

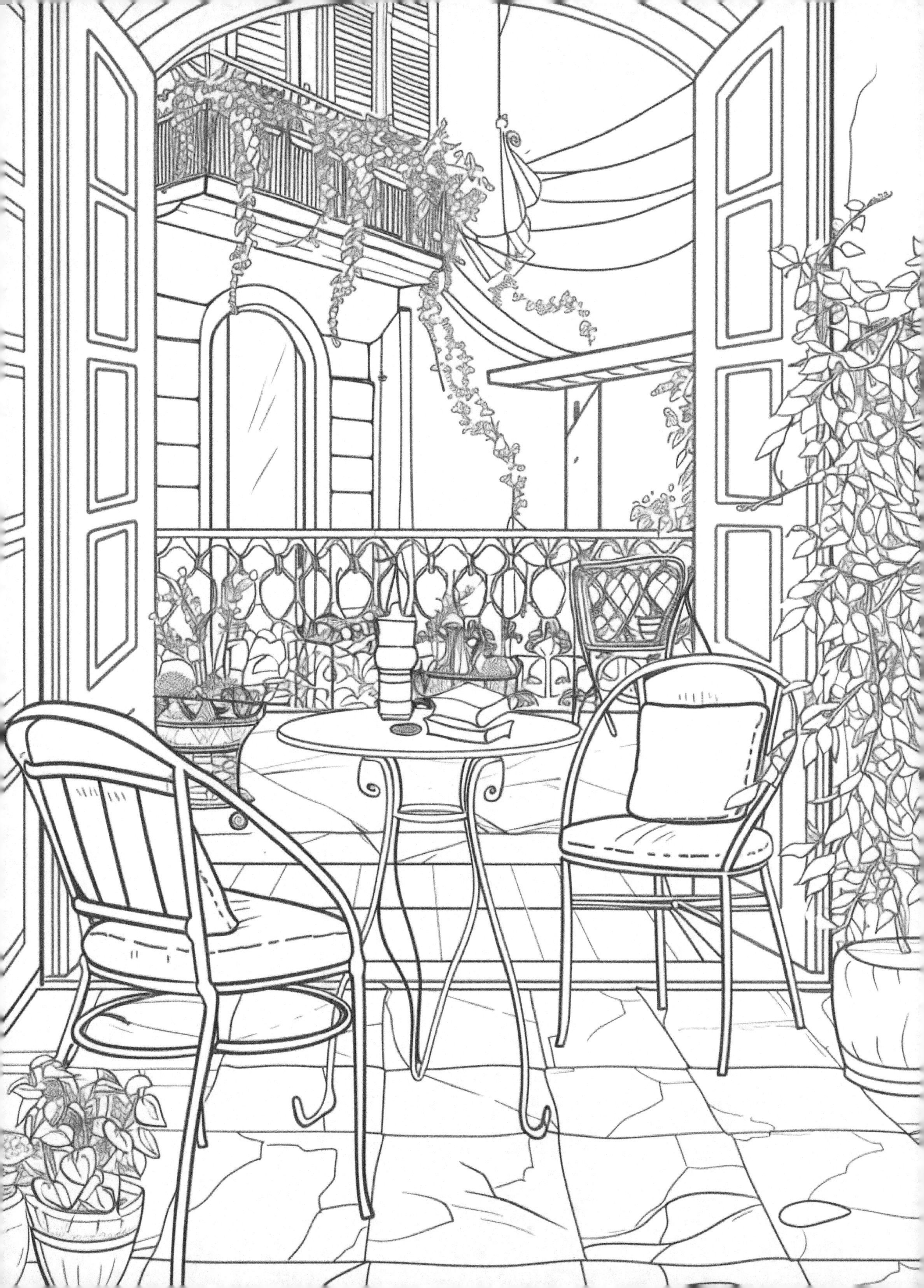

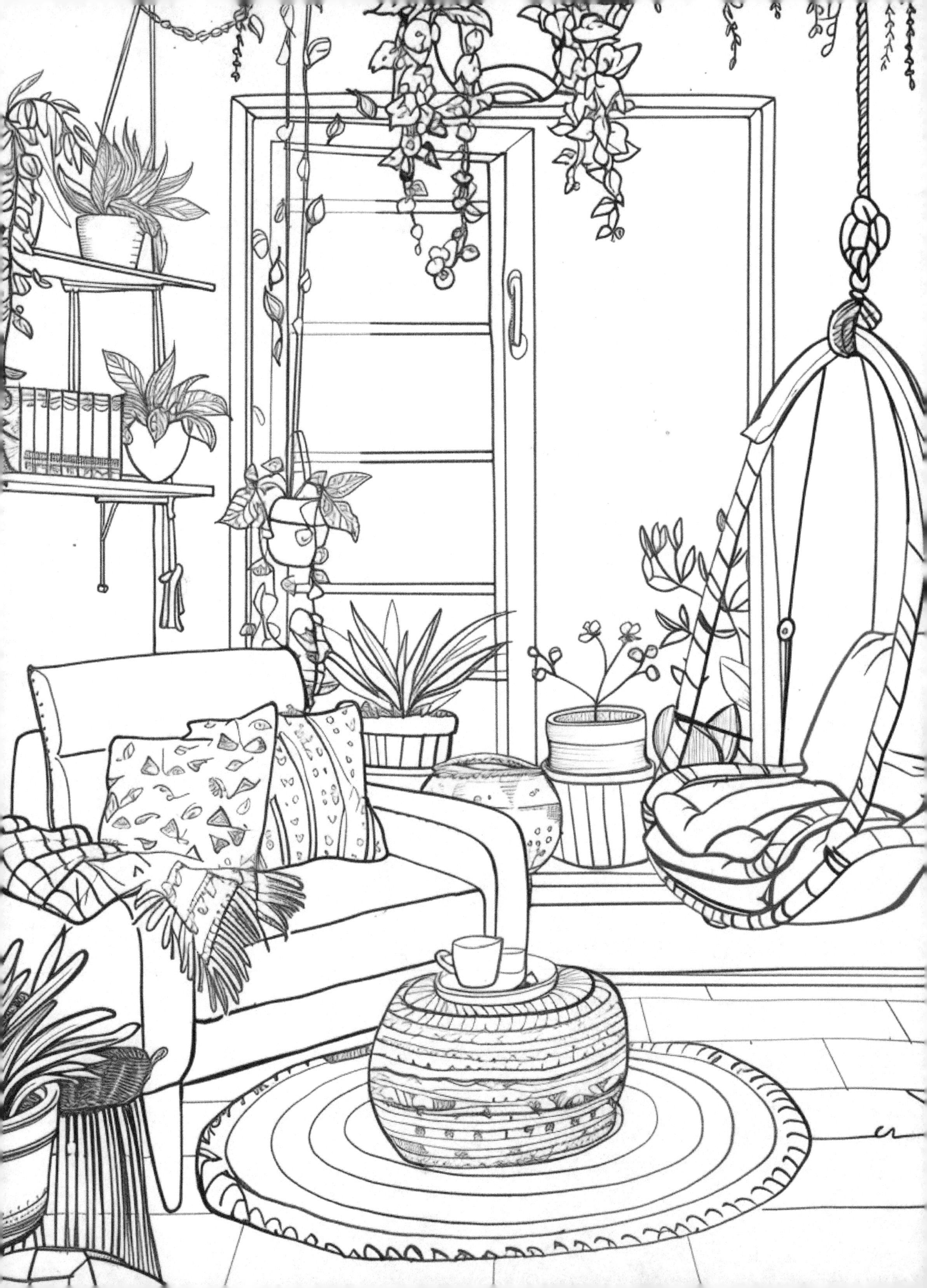

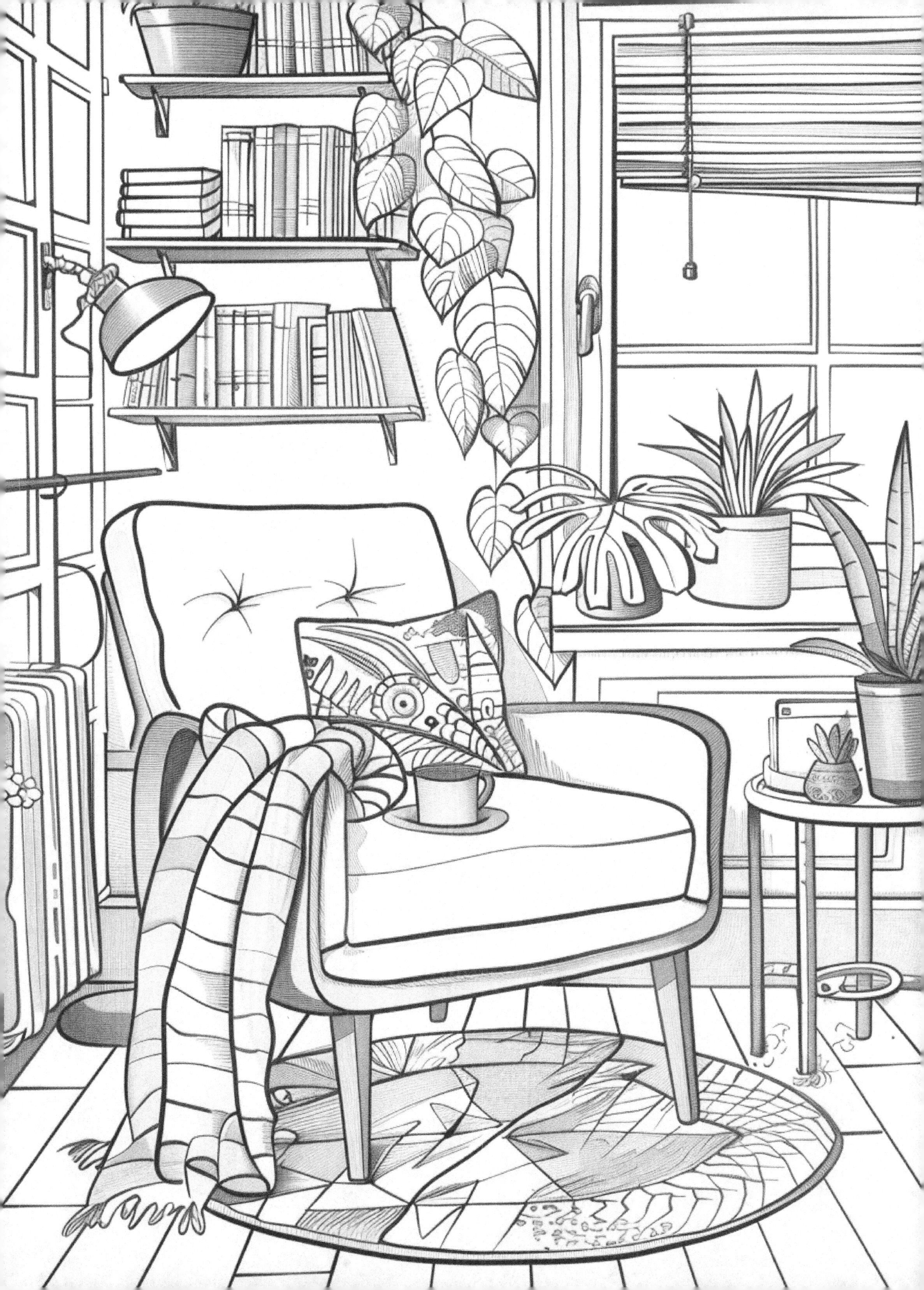

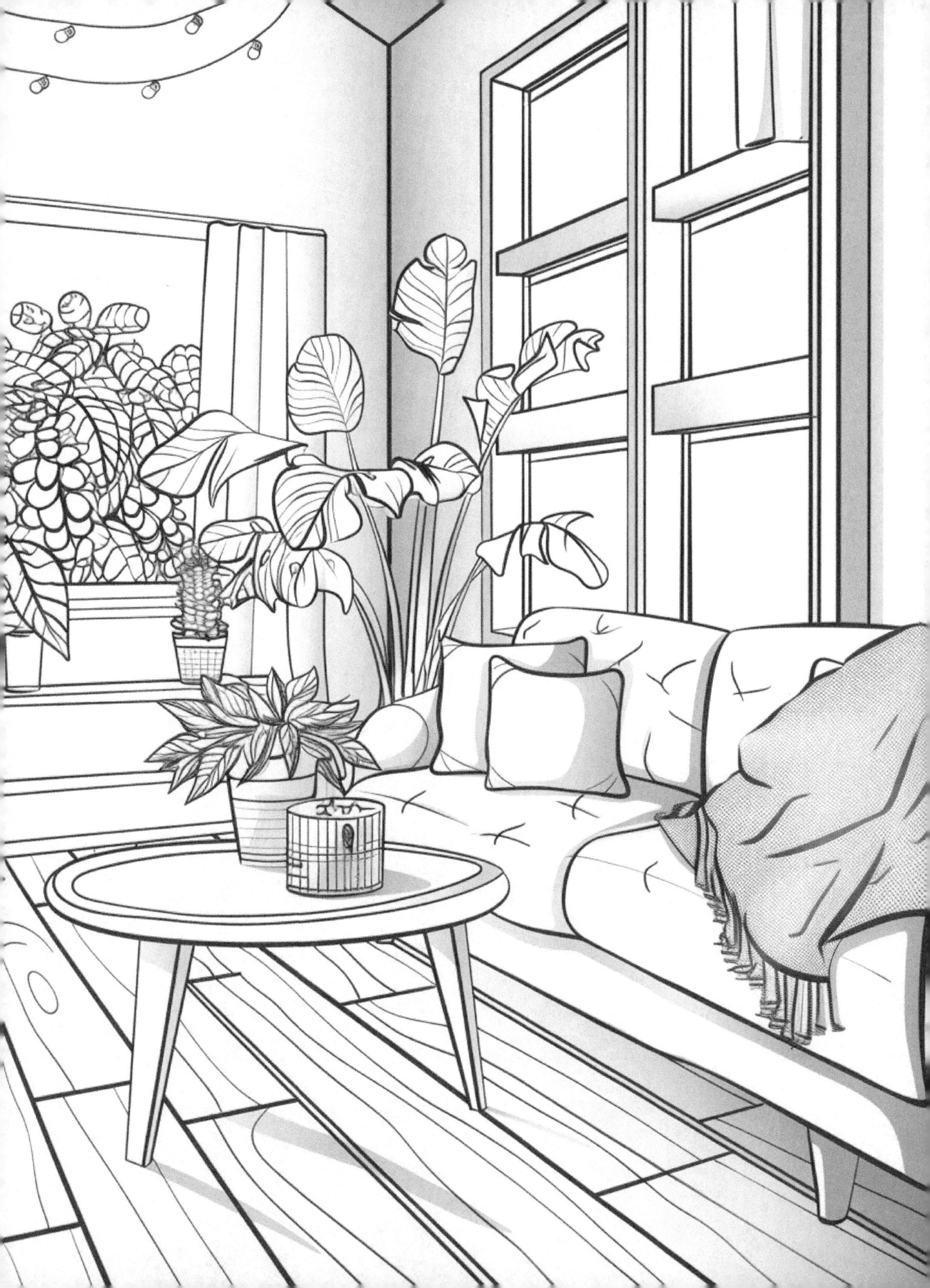

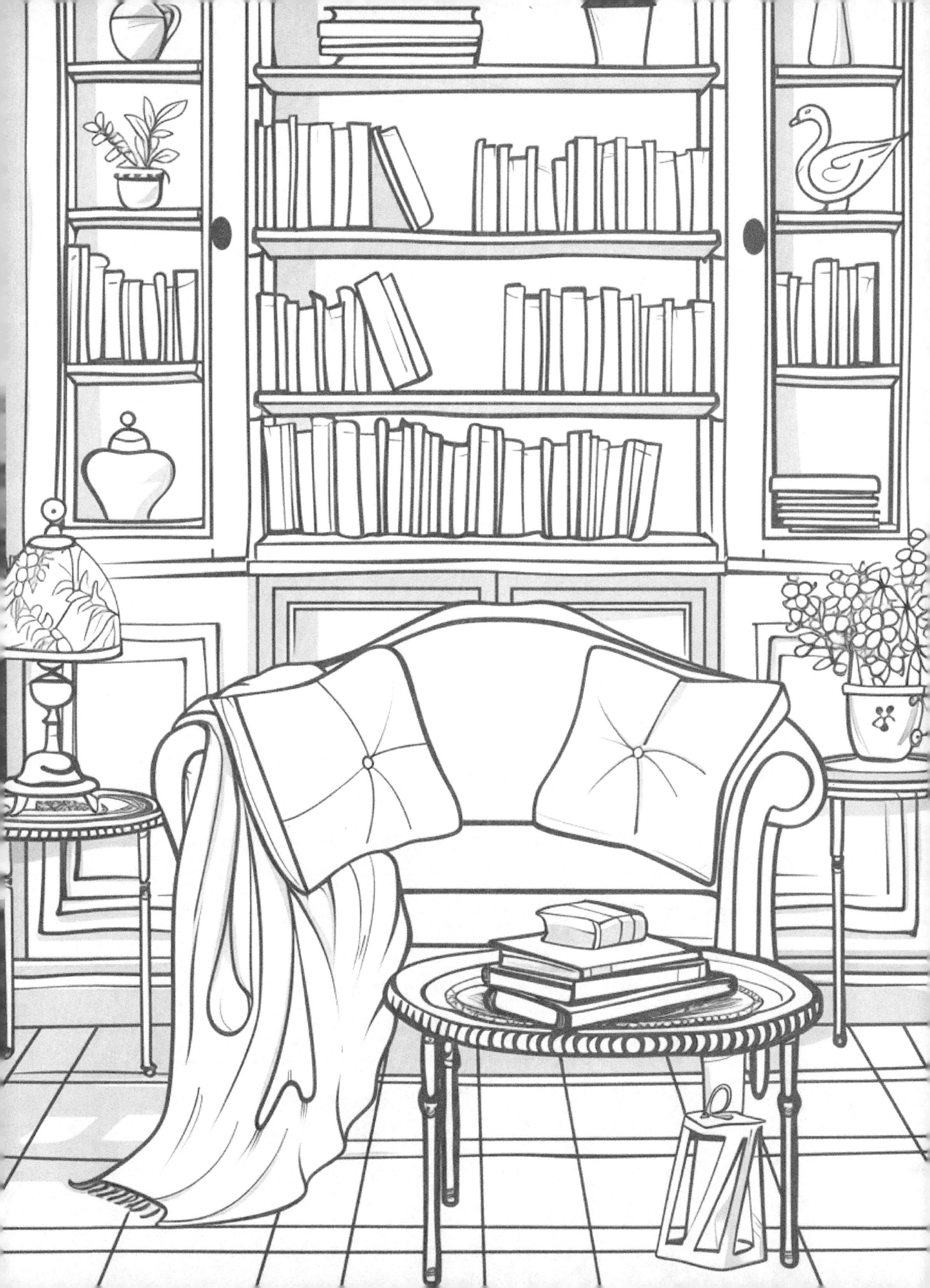

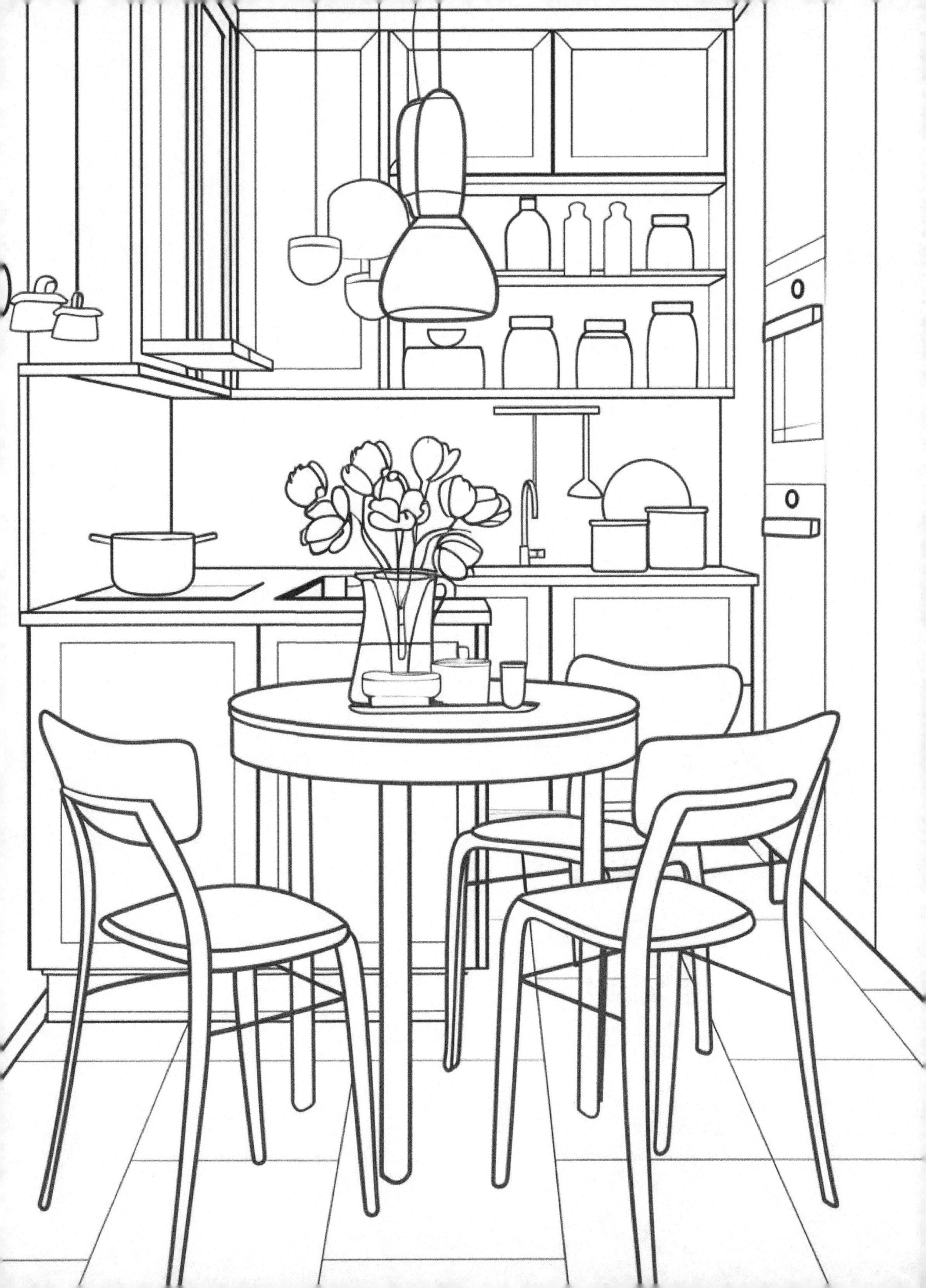

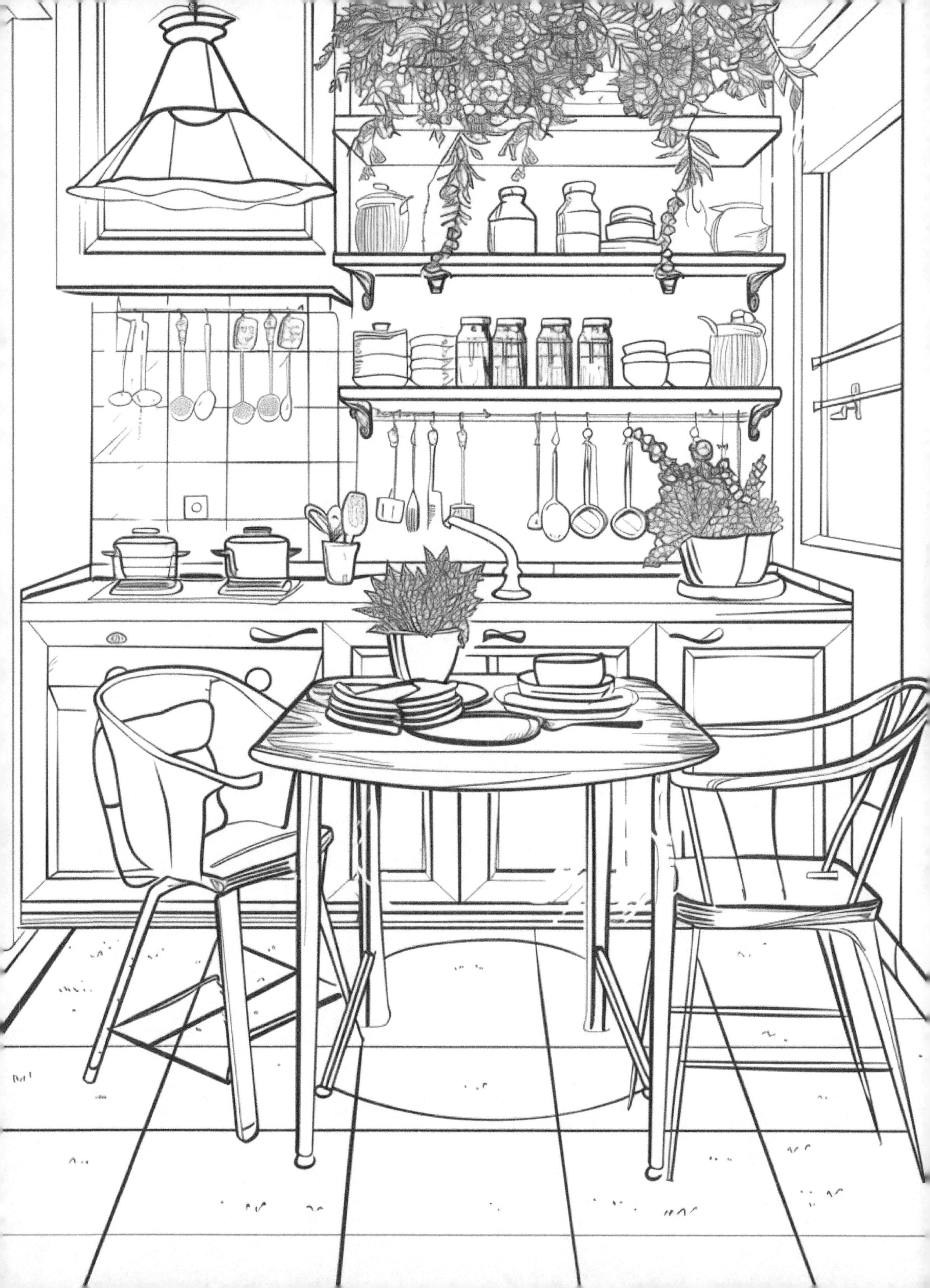

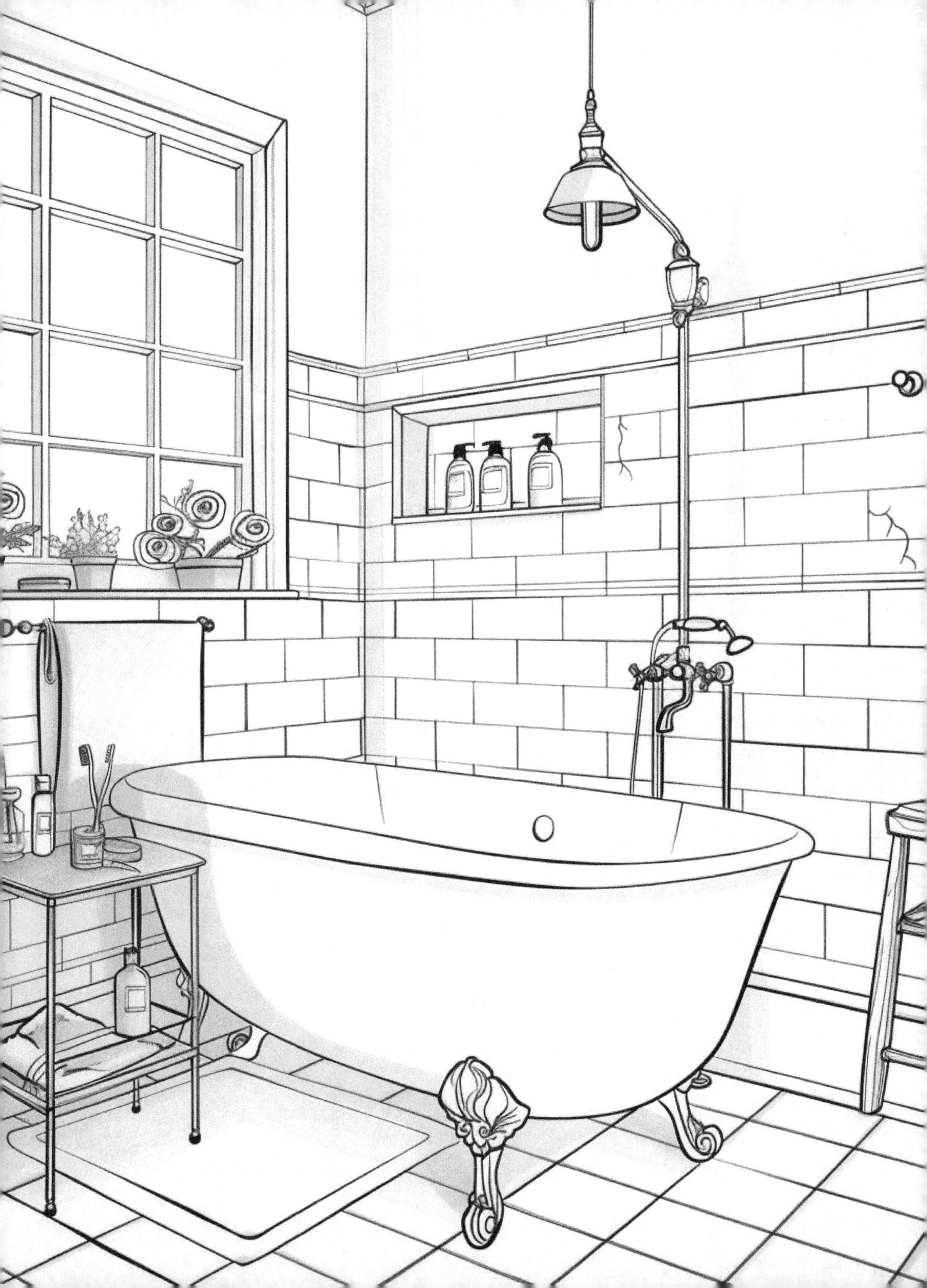

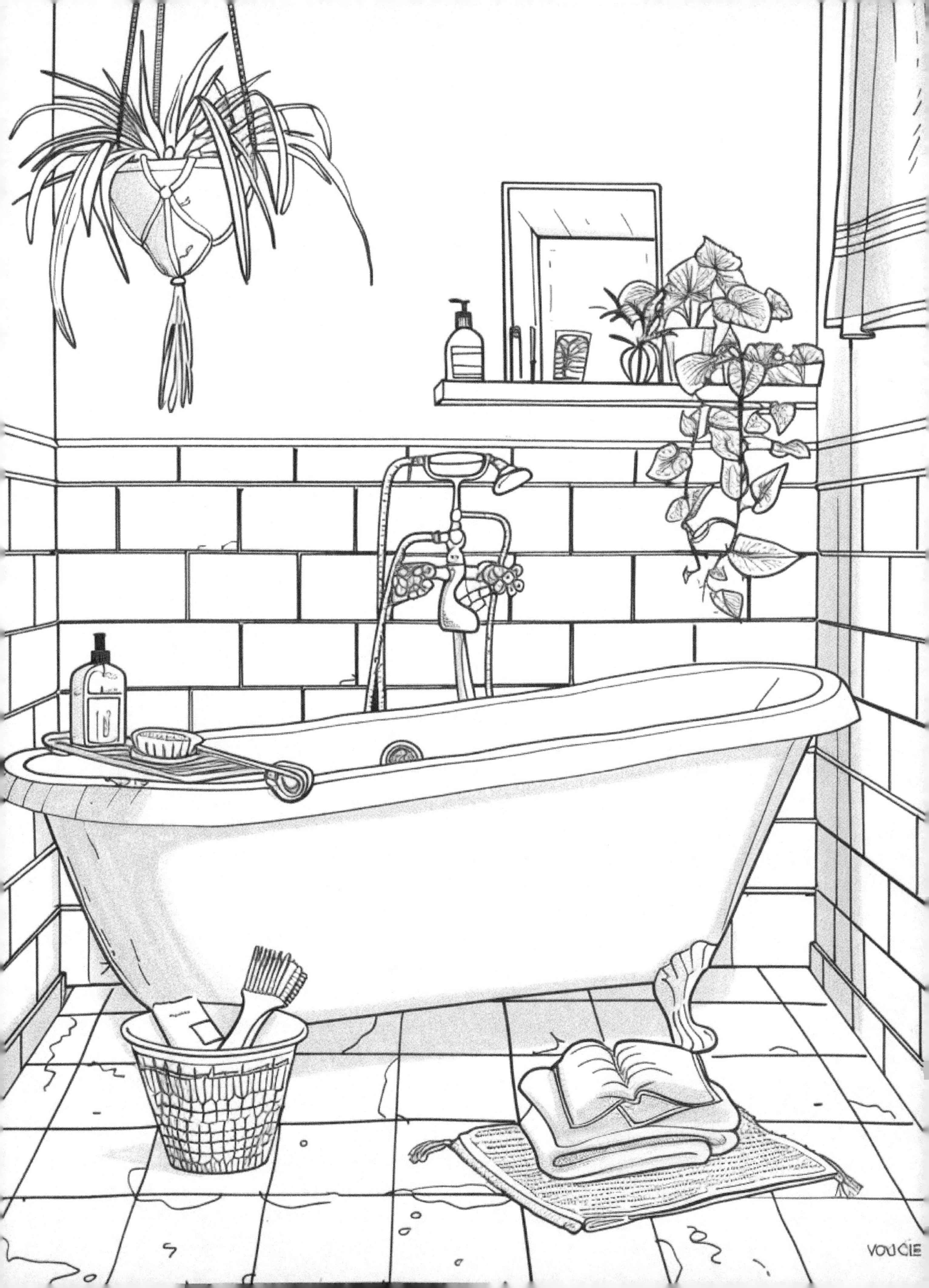
VOUCIE

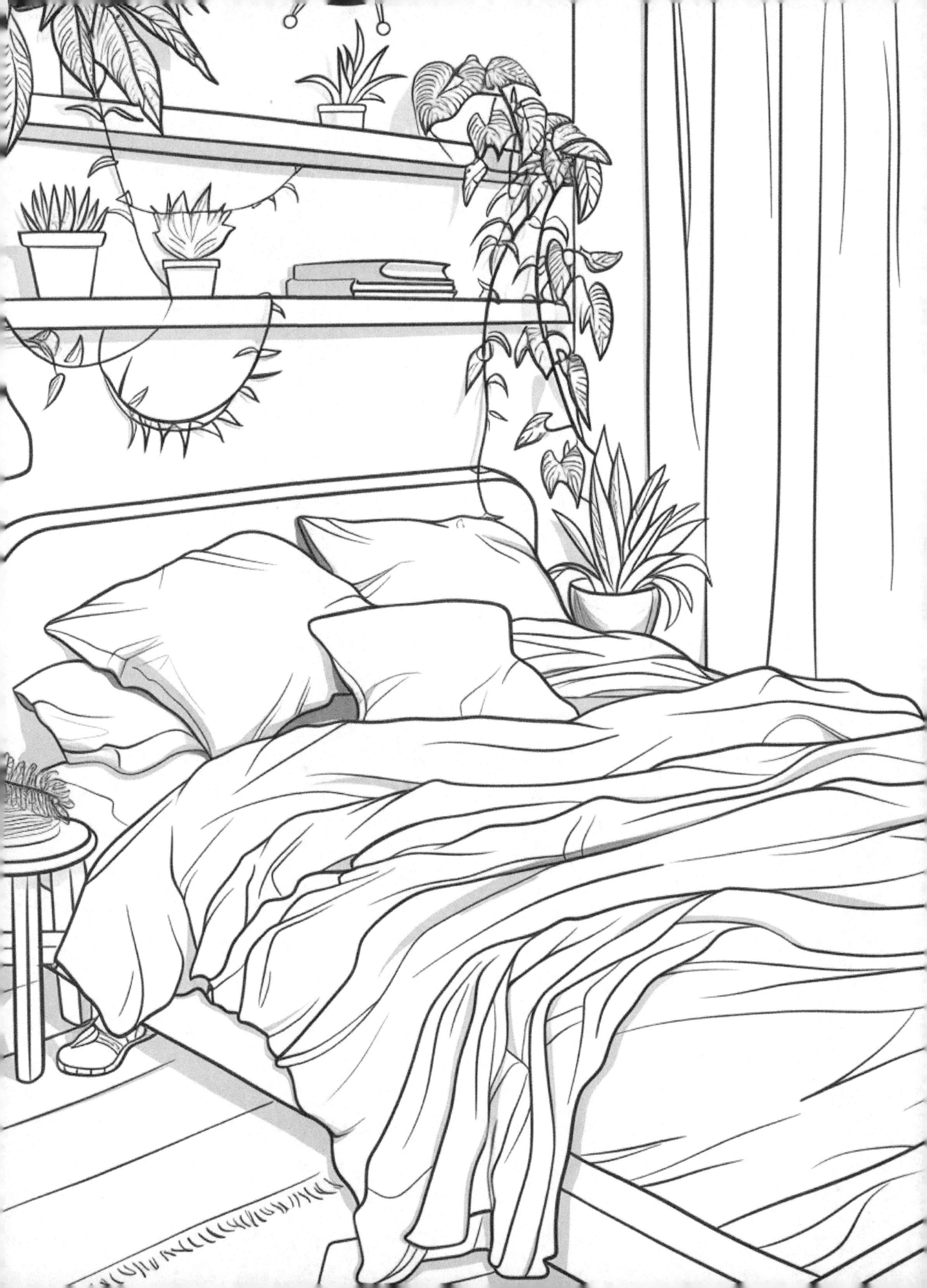

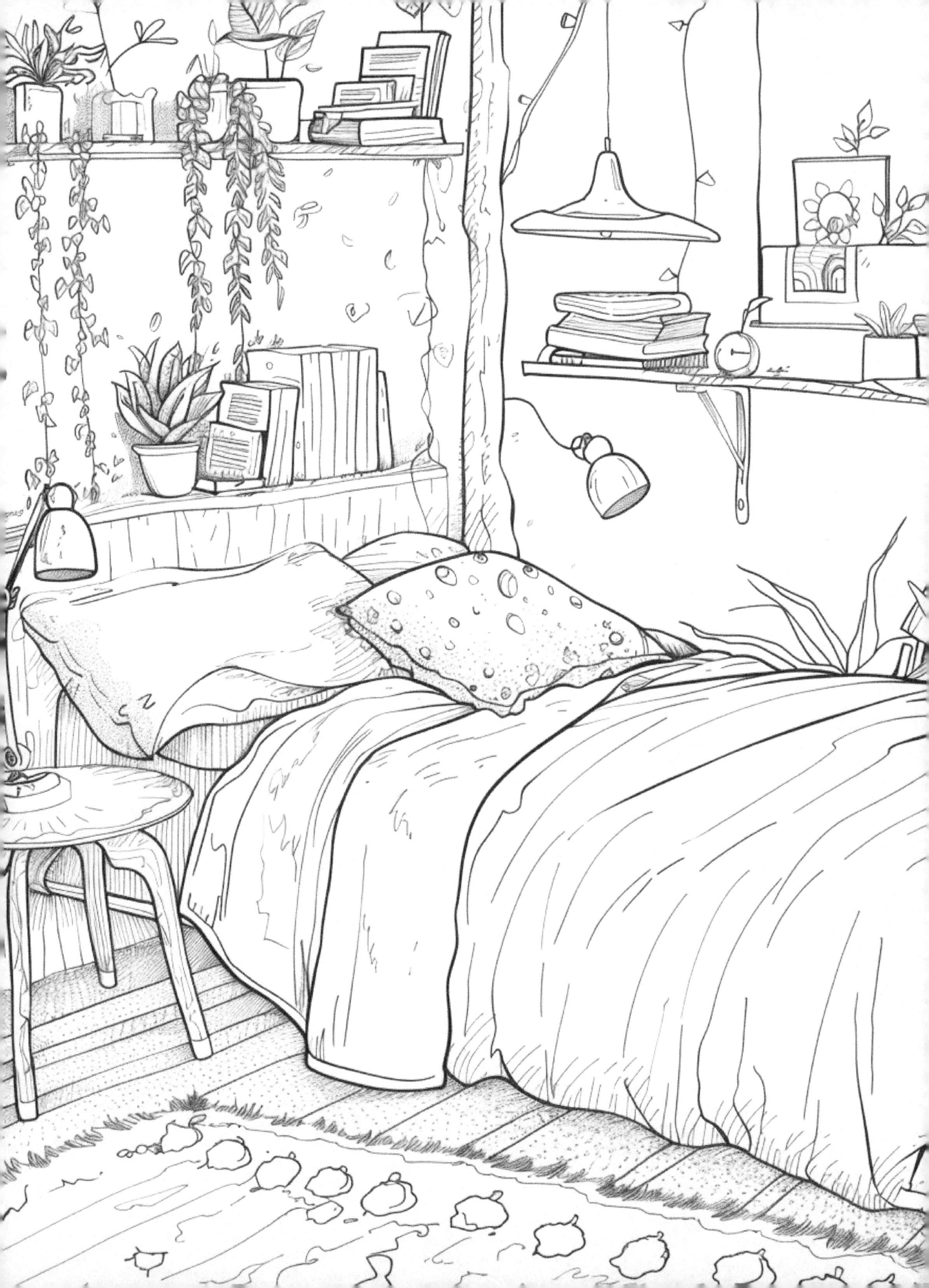

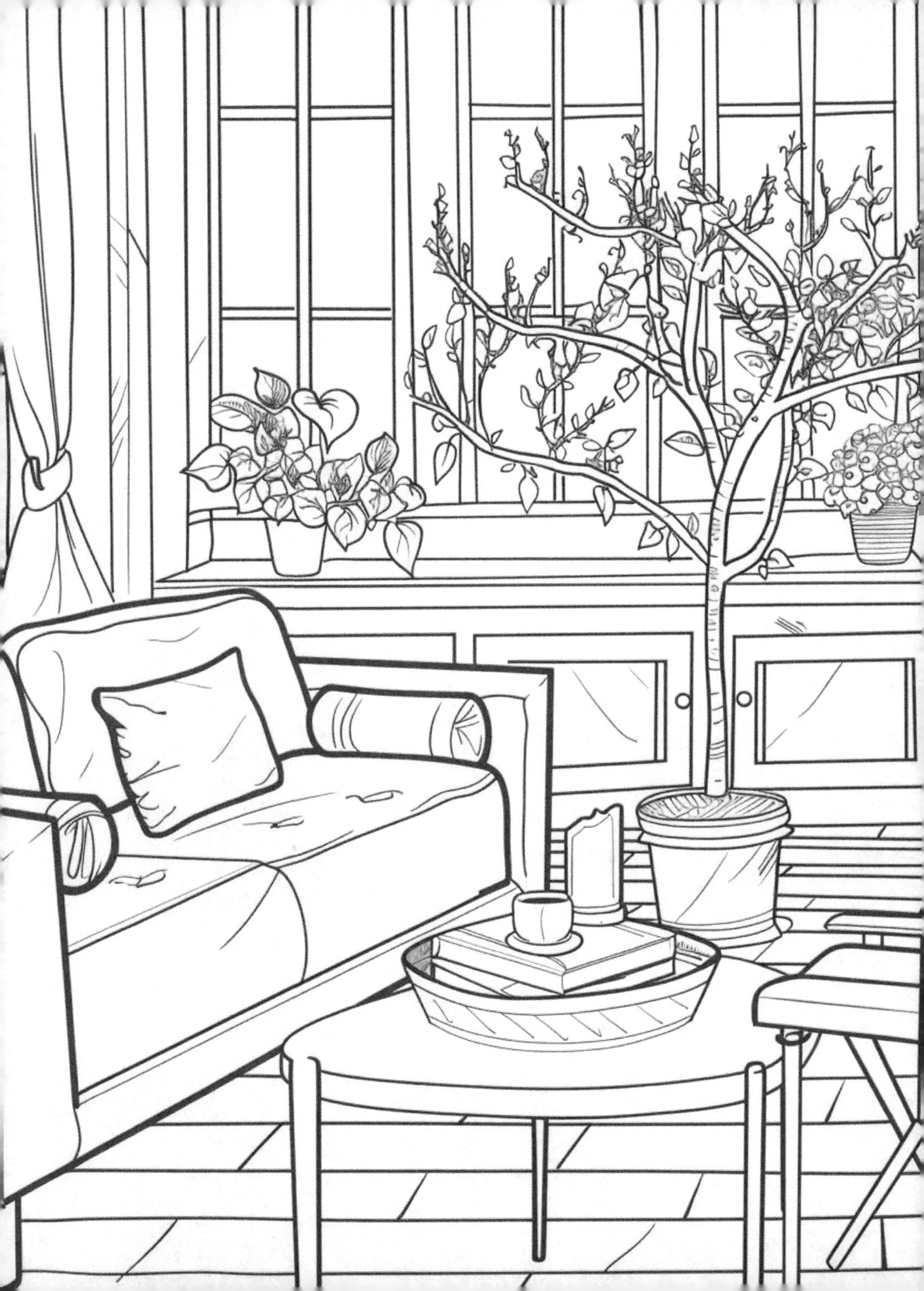

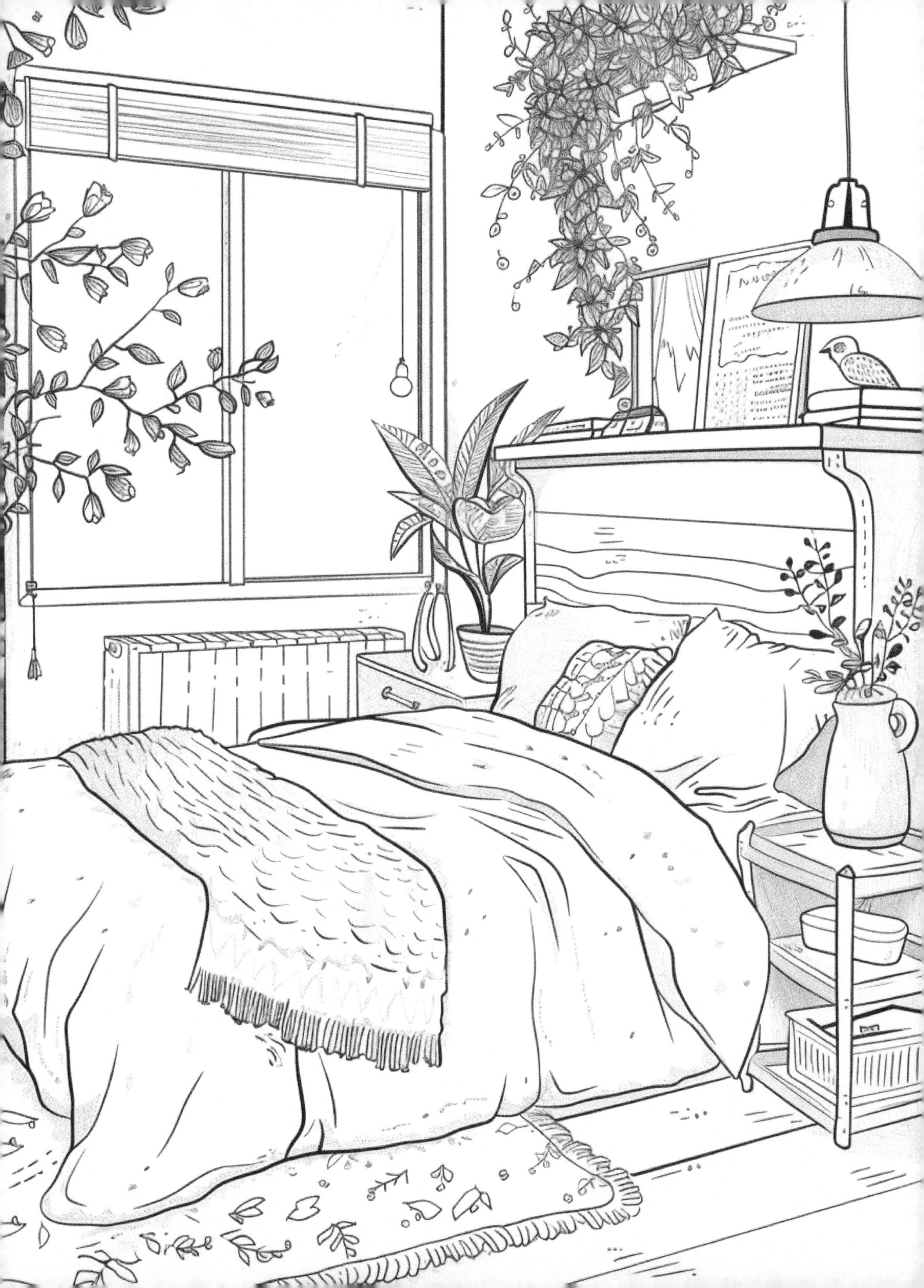

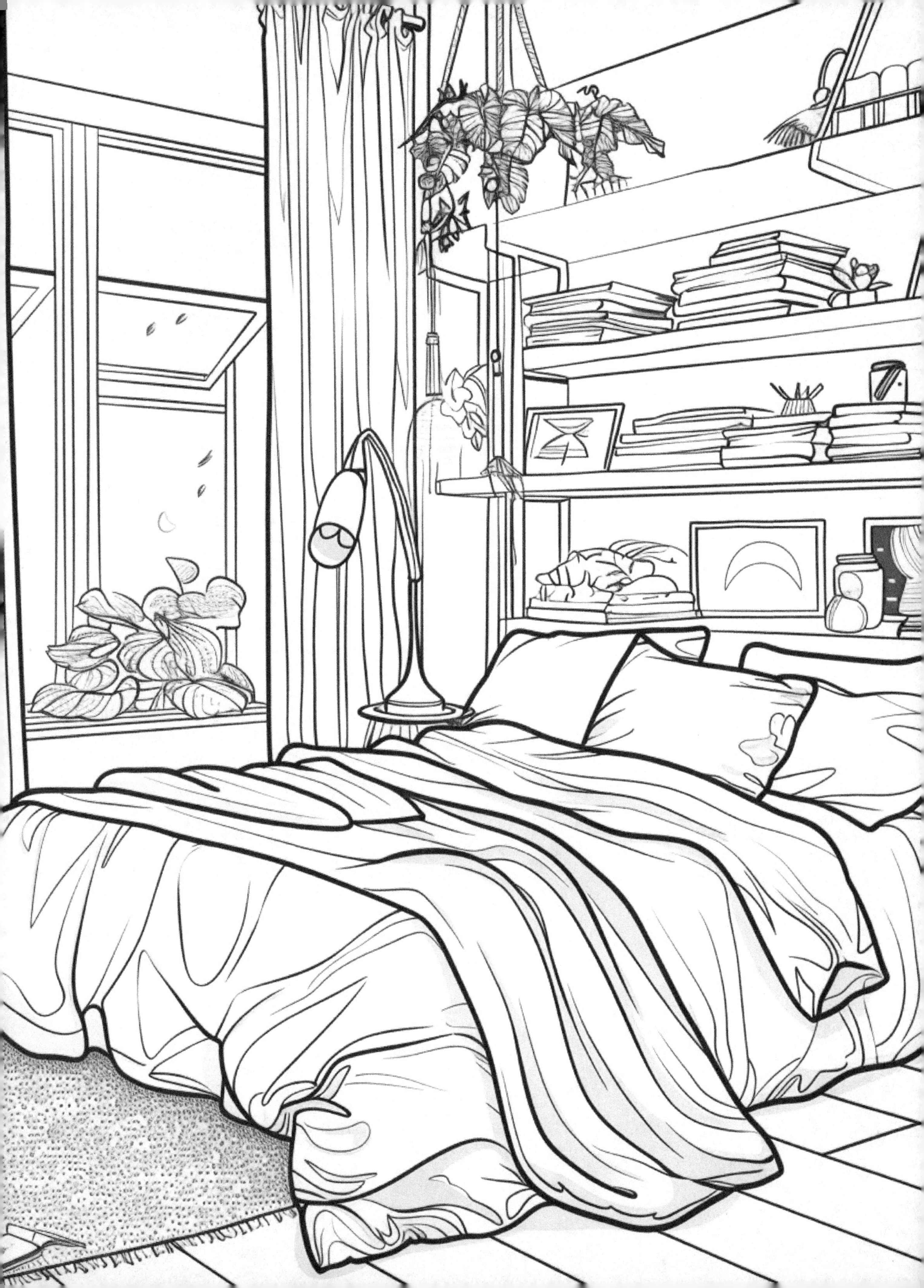

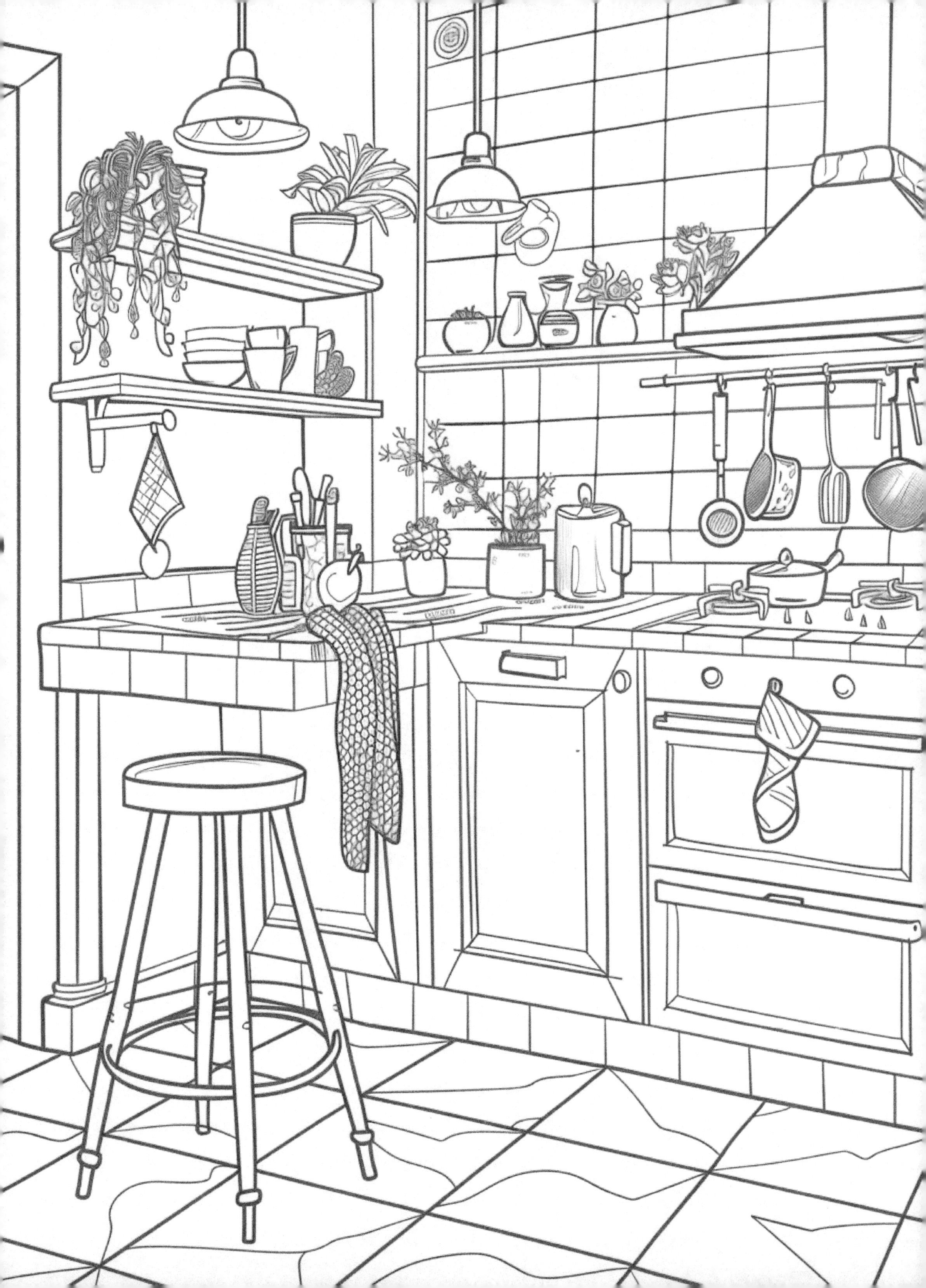

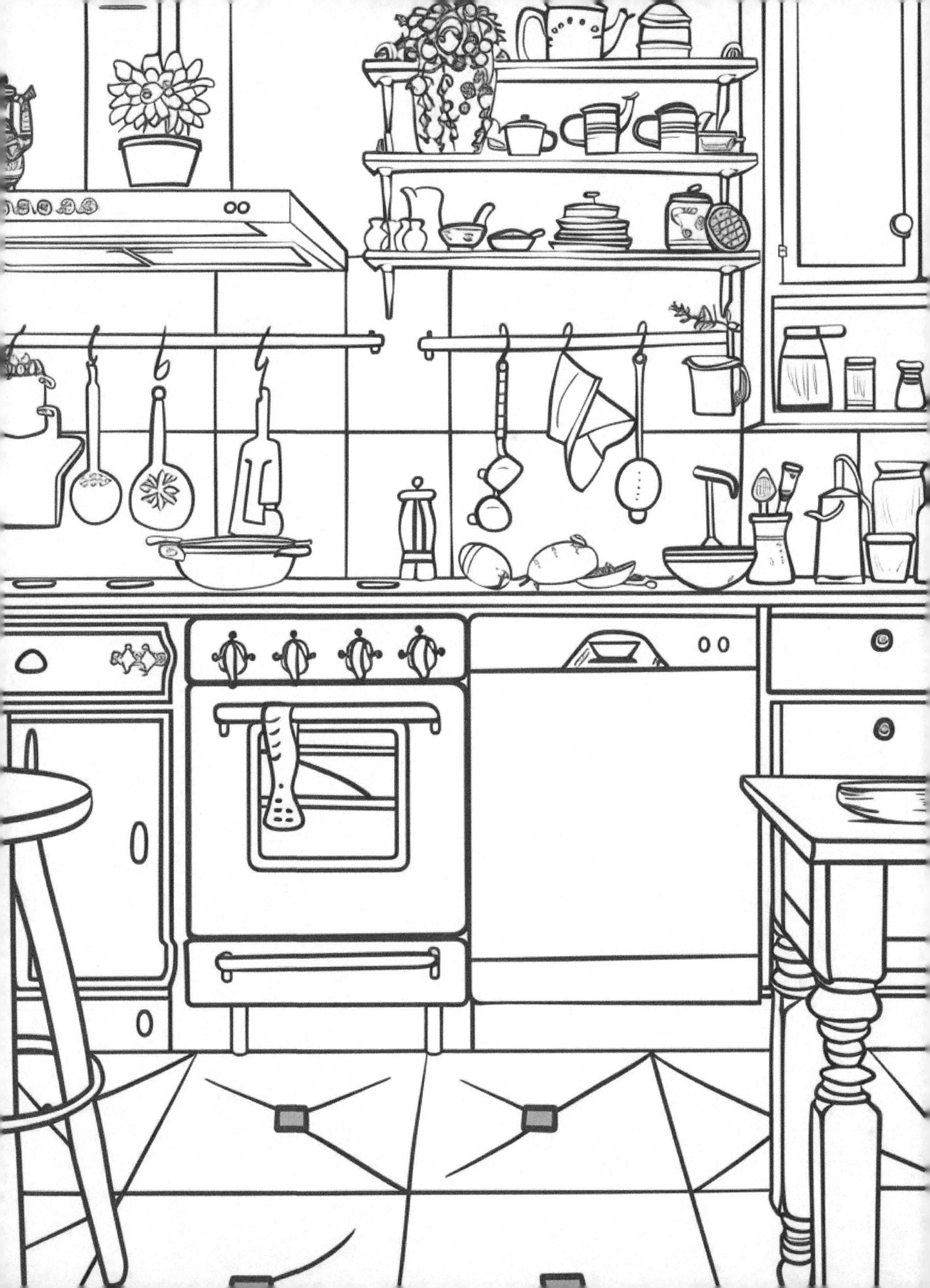

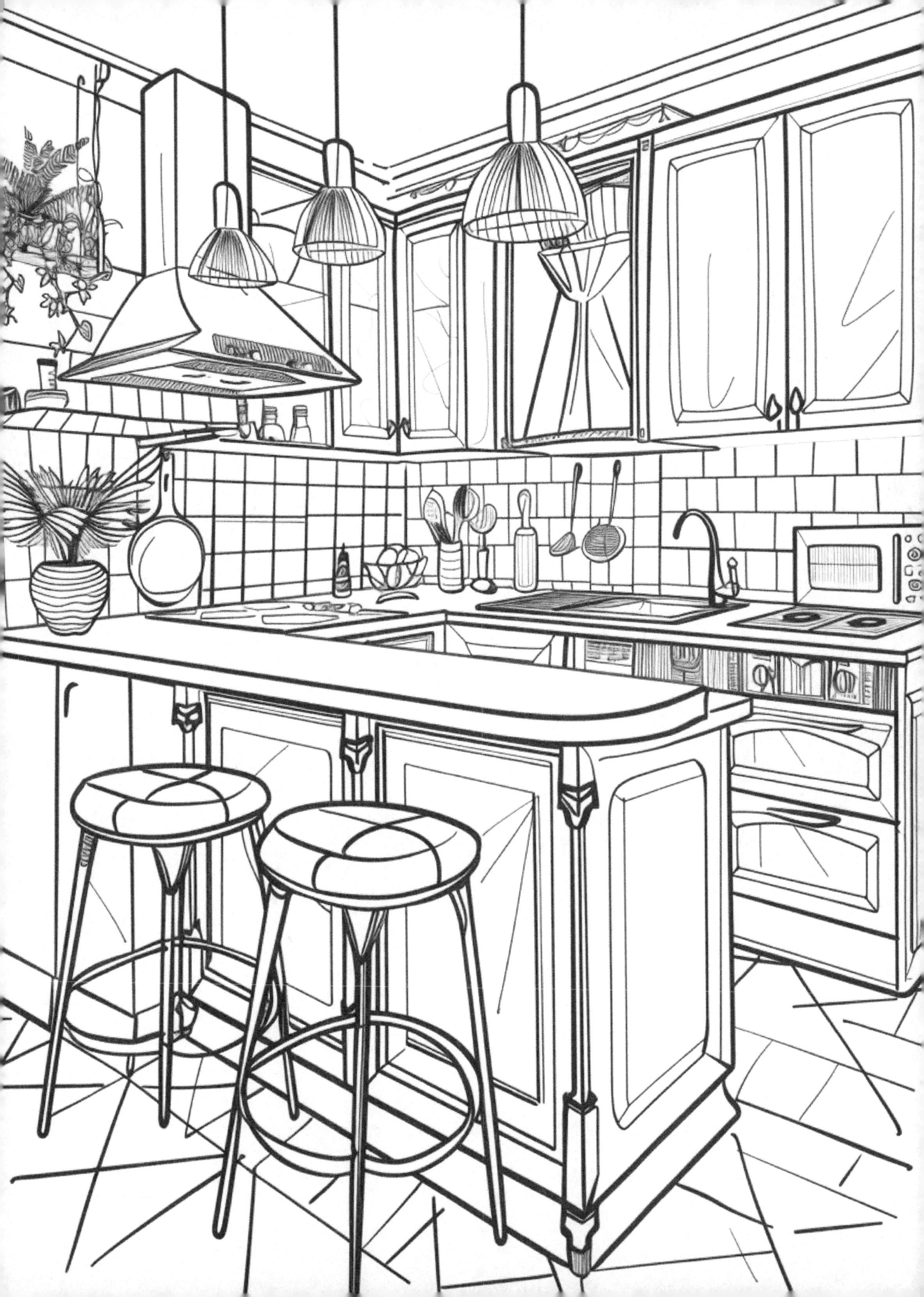

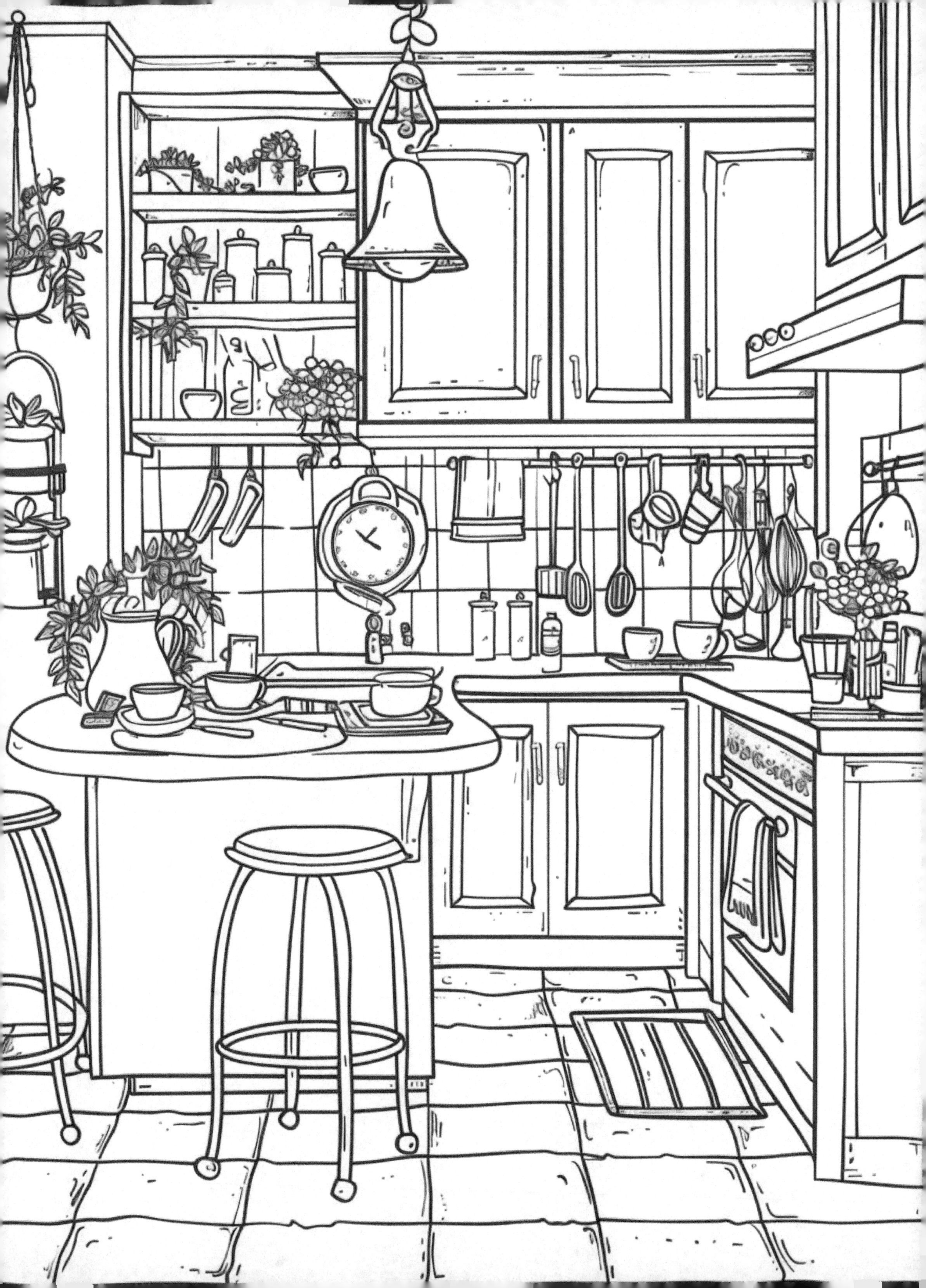

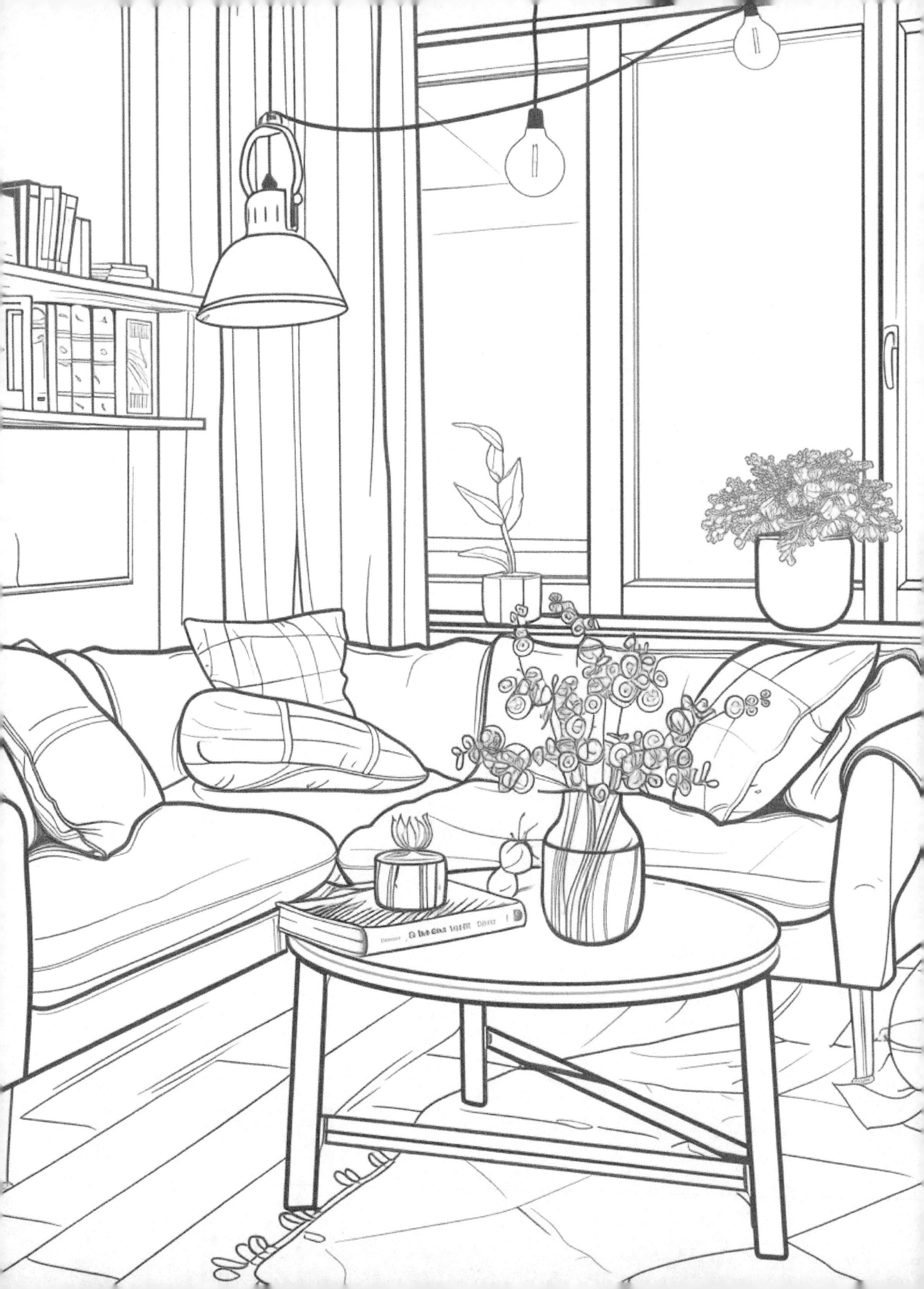

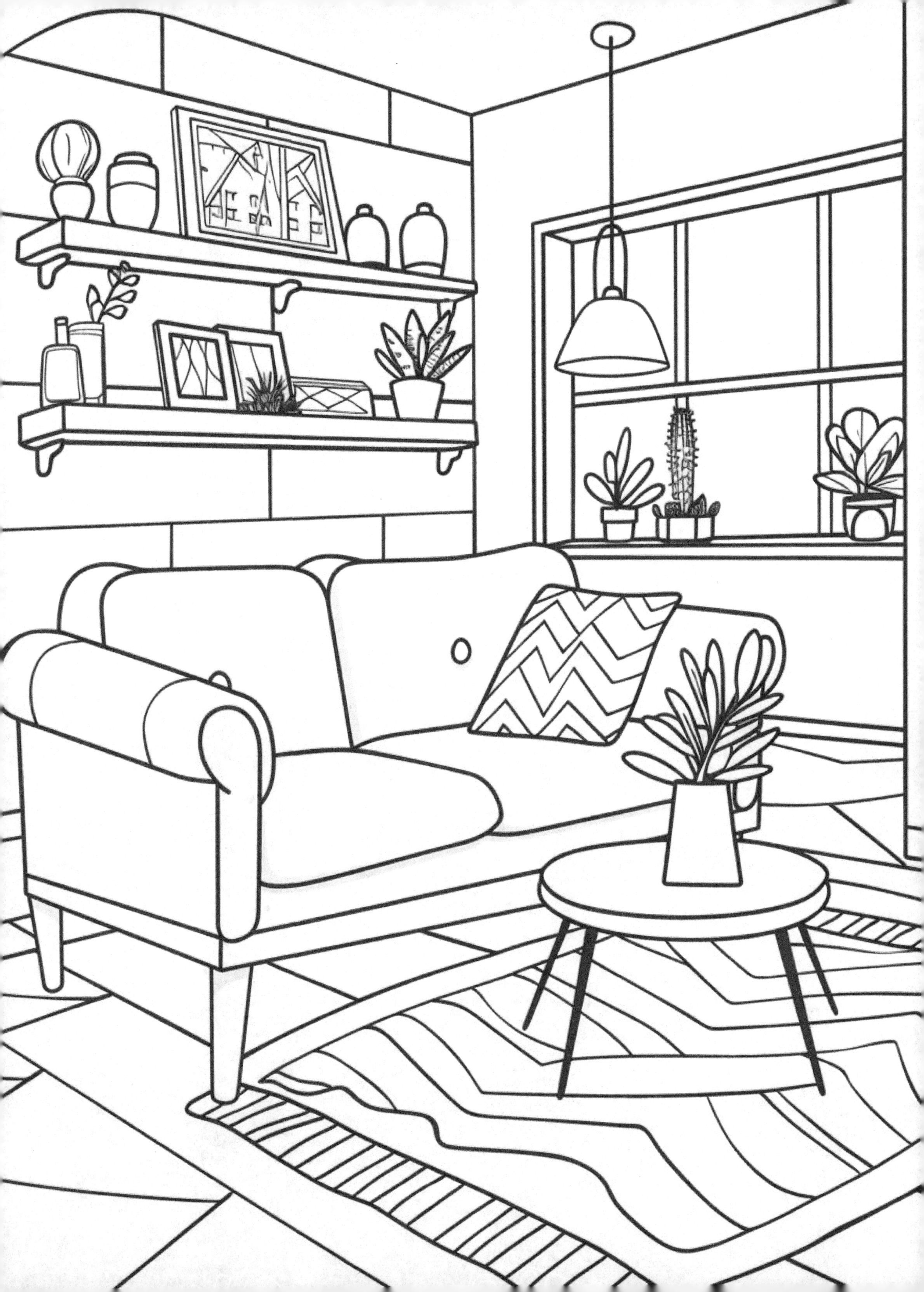

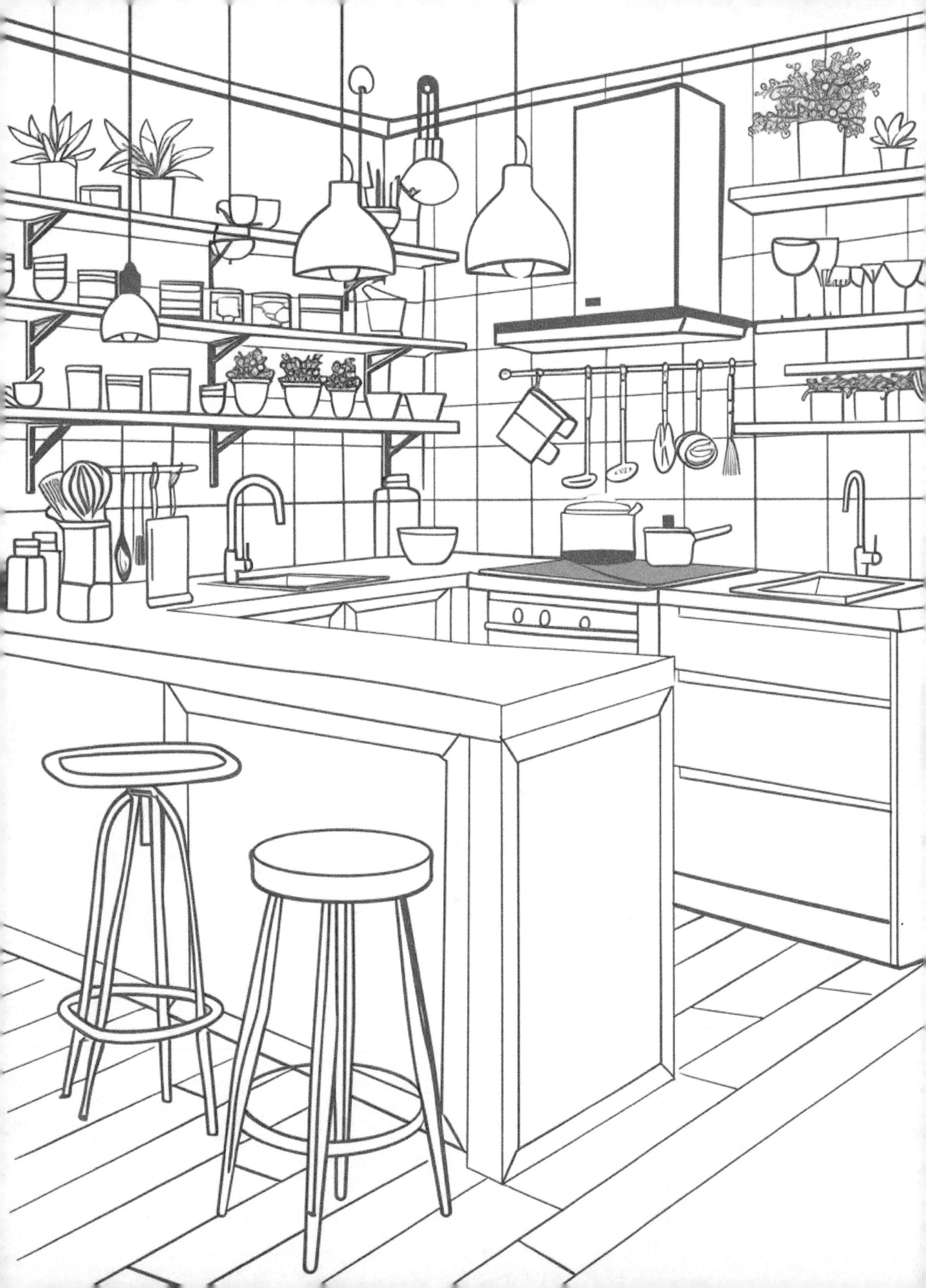

Made in United States
Orlando, FL
30 March 2025

59978333R00044